Love Your
LEFTOVERS

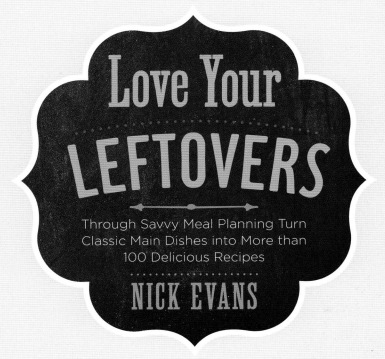

Love Your
LEFTOVERS

Through Savvy Meal Planning Turn
Classic Main Dishes into More than
100 Delicious Recipes

NICK EVANS

Guilford, Connecticut
An imprint of Globe Pequot Press

To buy books in quantity for corporate use
or incentives, call **(800) 962-0973**
or e-mail **premiums@GlobePequot.com.**

Lyons Press is an imprint of Globe Pequot Press.

Photographs by Nick Evans

Design: Sheryl. P. Kober
Project editor: Julie Marsh
Layout: Melissa Evarts

Library of Congress Cataloging-in-Publication Data

Evans, Nick, 1983—author.
Love your leftovers : through savvy meal planning turn classic main dishes into more than 100 delicious recipes / Nick Evans.
pages cm
Summary: "Nick Evans' philosophy is that homemade food is best and he is passionate about teaching people the value of a basic dish. The meal planning method in this book features a foundation dish that can be transformed into numerous other dishes throughout the week, saving you time and money, and leaving you with an impressive array of weeknight meals. This book will introduce you to dozens of possibilities for making your leftovers last, always striking the perfect balance between high quality food and low cost and effort"—Provided by publisher.
Includes index.
ISBN 978-0-7627-9142-2 (paperback)
1. Cooking (Leftovers) I. Title.
TX740.E835 2014
641.5'52—dc23
2013050236

Printed in the United States of America

10 9 8 7 6 5 4 3 2 1

This book is for my wife, Bets, who had to eat her way through multiple versions of the dishes in this book, some versions better than others. I also dedicate it to the lovely community of Macheesmo readers out there, who gave me the courage to write this sucker.

———————≈———————

CONTENTS

INTRODUCTION

I know what you're thinking: Another cookbook? Hasn't everything been cooked and booked by now?

Trust me, I've thought the same thing while browsing the new cookbooks on Amazon or in the local bookstore. With the explosion of celebrity chefs and food blogs, cookbooks seem to be a dime a dozen. (If only they were that cheap!)

The shocking thing about all of these cookbooks is that most of them are surprisingly good. The authors spend a huge amount of time developing recipes, taking photographs, and writing useful descriptions. Flip to any page in any number of cookbooks, and you'll find a recipe that you can successfully follow to make a great dish. I have dozens and dozens of cookbooks on my shelves that are filled with good recipes.

But the truth is that I rarely open them.

I've come down with a serious case of what I call "cookbook fatigue." I have all of these fantastic books that I know contain delicious recipes, but when it comes down to planning my weekly meal schedule, I don't want to spend a lot of time combing through them.

So I started brainstorming a way to plan my weekly meals without scavenging through dozens of books. That brainstorm led to this book!

When I began working on this project, I wanted to produce more than just a collection of random recipes; I wanted to give you a book that would help you plan meals and make efficient use of both your time and budget.

I started by thinking about how efficient cooks use leftovers to their advantage. You may not know this, but restaurants frequently repurpose what are essentially leftovers into daily specials or other dishes. They'll make one dish, serve it, and then make something completely different with the leftovers on day two. Roasted chickens become chicken tortilla soup. Baked potatoes morph into gnocchi. Meanwhile all of us home cooks have been thinking we have to start from scratch each and every day.

I found there are certain dishes that are not only good meals in their own right but also make solid starting points for other equally good dishes. These dishes are the basis for the fourteen recipe chapters in this book. They can almost all be part of a meal as is on day one, but then the leftovers can easily be used for other dishes throughout the week. Those secondary dishes take less time and money to make because much of the work is already done. These are the types of dishes that I recommend people incorporate into their weekly meal plans.

The leftovers cooking philosophy is simply to make large batches of these main dishes when you have the time and then use the leftovers to make new meals throughout the week. When you shift your thinking toward preparing meals that build off one another, you'll find it opens up a whole world of new dishes that once seemed out of reach.

After I got the hang of meal planning using this leftover method, I realized I was making things like homemade chicken and dumplings on a Tuesday in under an hour, and it tasted like I'd been slaving away all day.

Finding the Time to Cook

I believe cooking is an incredibly important skill for anyone who cares about feeding his or her friends and family good, healthy meals. Once you get the hang of it, you can save money, eat healthier, and possibly (just possibly) have fun.

That said, I'm not one of those people who's going to pull your leg and tell you that this book is filled with quick meals that take no time at all. Nope. Some of these recipes do take time, and I hope that, as you explore what's here, you'll find time to try them. If you've read my blog, Macheesmo.com, you'll know that I'm very upfront about the work a dish requires. You won't find any surprises here, either. If I say a dish takes thirty minutes, that means it took thirty minutes for me to make in my home kitchen with no help and most likely with some distractions. But I won't lie. There are some recipes in this book that have the word "hours" in the cook time.

Take a deep breath. You can make it happen. You'll be well rewarded.

Using This Book

Each of the fourteen recipe chapters in this book begins with a main dish. In general these are the dishes that take the longest to cook, although a few will be ready in under an hour. These main dishes store easily, keep well, and can be used later to make the subsequent recipes in a given chapter.

Now, you don't necessarily need to make the main dish to make the related dishes in any given chapter. I encourage you to get creative. For example, in the roast chicken chapter, you can use any leftover chicken, or you can buy a rotisserie chicken and use that for the supporting recipes. Likewise, the marinara recipes work great with any store-bought variety of marinara. You get the idea.

But ideally you can spend some time on a lazy Sunday to make a main dish or two, and then your meals for the week will pretty much plan themselves. I've tried to vary the recipes in each chapter by offering options for breakfast, lunch, and dinner, and I've also aimed to cover a range of cuisines. So, just like in a restaurant, you'll be using leftovers, but you'll be making new, tasty dishes with them.

Depending on the dish and your family size, you may want to consider doubling the main recipes to really maximize the idea. That should leave you plenty to feed a family and also have some leftovers to use in the other recipes.

Crowd-Sourced Testing

One aspect of this book that I'm really proud of is the testing that each recipe underwent. Not only did I make all the recipes multiple times for family and friends, but I also recruited a team of recipe testers from all over the United States (and a few other countries) to help test out the recipes. These volunteer recipe testers did a fantastic service to this book. Almost every single recipe was tweaked based on comments from these testers, and I feel confident that you'll have success with the recipes because of the work that went into testing them.

CHAPTER 1

KITCHEN AND PANTRY BASICS

It's no secret that you're going to need some equipment if you plan on cooking regularly at home. Luckily, a good number of the recipes in this book use essentially the same basic items. Before you dive into the recipes, take a look at the equipment and pantry lists in this chapter. If you have these things on hand, you can make pretty much every recipe in the book, and if you don't, you may want to consider purchasing a few of them to make your life easier.

Equipment Basics

I do not recommend visiting your local kitchen equipment store and buying all this stuff in one trip. Start with the basics, and as you try new recipes, you can slowly add on to your kitchen equipment if needed. This equipment list is roughly in order of what I consider to be most important.

- Dutch oven—A large cast-iron enameled dutch oven is an invaluable kitchen tool. You can use it on the stovetop or in the oven and make a wide variety of things (including bread) with it. I recommend at least a 5-quart variety. I would advise getting a dutch oven before you get a large (4-quart) pot.

- Cast-iron skillet—As your first piece of cooking equipment, I usually advise the purchase of a dutch oven and a cast-iron skillet. They are just universally useful. Start with a 12-inch skillet.

- Chef's knife—I prefer a 10-inch chef's knife. Get the nicest knife you can afford, since you'll be using it a lot if you begin cooking more frequently. Invest in a honing steel as well to keep it sharp.

- Paring knife—There's no need for anything fancy here. I usually grab a $15 variety and trade it out every year or two.

- Various pots—You don't need a huge line of pots. I have three different pots that I use for everything: 4-quart, 2½-quart, and ½-quart sizes.

- Metal mixing bowls—These come in a variety of sizes, and you can usually pick up a sturdy set for $30 to $40. I use mine every day.

- **Glass storage containers**—I like really sturdy containers for leftovers to keep food as fresh as possible for as long as possible. Glass makes it easy to reheat in the microwave, if needed, and is also really easy to clean. They are a bit more expensive but worth the investment.

- **Sheet pans**—I use baking sheets almost daily. Depending on your oven size, you can get the half sheet (13 x 18-inch) or the quarter sheet (9 x 13-inch) size.

- **Wok or large skillet**—If you make a lot of stir-fries, it might be worth it to invest in a nice wok, but a large skillet can get the job done in most cases.

- **Baking dishes**—A wide variety is nice, but at a minimum I recommend a 9 x 13-inch and an 8 x 8-inch dish. A few mid-range casserole dishes like a 2½-quart dish are helpful.

- **Thermometers**—I always recommend that people have two types of thermometers in their kitchens: meat thermometers and deep-fry thermometers. Both are invaluable and cost just a few bucks. An oven thermometer also helps if you are grilling a lot, to make sure your grill is the right temperature.

- **Tongs**—This might be the thing I use the most in the kitchen. They're perfect for flipping meat and grabbing pasta. I think a 12-inch length is just fine.

- **Spice grinder**—Buying ground spices is more convenient, but they charge you for that convenience. Whole spices are cheaper and keep for years. Make the switch to grinding your own if you can. Personally, I like to use a mortar and pestle for small batches of spices.

- **Potato masher**—I use mine for more than just potatoes. I also use it to speed up a tomato sauce, for example, as it cooks down.

- **Microplane grater**—Used for zesting fruit and also for grating super-fine Parmesan cheese and other hard cheeses. For a few bucks, it's a great kitchen tool.

- **Wire mesh strainer**—It has much smaller holes than a colander and works great to drain and rinse a can of beans or strain your ice cream custard so it's silky smooth.

- **Blender**—Important for smoothies, sauces, and the occasional milkshake. An immersion blender makes soup preparation a breeze.

- **Serrated bread knife**—If you start making homemade bread a lot, you'll want a good serrated knife to slice it and not make a mess of your pretty loaf. This knife is also good for slicing tomatoes and sandwiches.

- **Roasting pan**—Used for roasting chickens and bones for homemade stocks. I like a sturdy metal one with high walls. If you're working on acquiring kitchen equipment, you can almost always just use a 9 x 13-inch baking dish for this in a pinch.

- **Muffin tin**—Muffins are the obvious choice, but I also use mine for lots of savory dishes and freeze stuff in them for easy portion control.

- **Ramekins**—A few ramekins of various sizes are always helpful. I like to have four 7-ounce ramekins on hand for easy desserts. If you don't have ramekins, however, you can also adapt most recipes for use with a muffin tin.

- **Food processor**—This is solidly in the would-be-nice category. I survived without one for years and years, but I appreciate it now that I have it.

- **Grill or grill pan**—Grilling food is a healthy way to prepare it. It's great to have one in your preparation arsenal.

- **Loaf pan**—This is perfect for meatloaf or sandwich bread. You'll find lots of uses once you have it handy. A 9 x 5-inch size is standard.

- **Pie pan**—Pie pans work for more than just pies. I often use mine for frittatas and quiches.

- **12-quart stockpot**—If you get into the habit of making a lot of homemade stocks, which is a fairly awesome habit to get into, you'll want a sturdy, large stockpot.

- **Pizza stone and peel**—If you make pizza more than a few times a year (and you should be doing this), it's probably worth it to invest in a decent stone that you can heat in the oven and a peel so you can slide your pizza (or calzones) right onto the hot stone.

- **Ice cream maker**—This is far from an essential piece of kitchen gear, unless you happen to love ice cream. Then you need one!

- **Slow cooker**—If you're a busy person—and who isn't—a slow cooker is your best friend. Many recipes that require long cook times can be easily adapted for the slow cooker, so you can make them while you are at work!

- **Miscellaneous gear**—One good flat spatula, a dough scraper, wooden spoons, a cheese grater, ice cream scooper, slotted spoon, colander, whisk, ladle, parchment paper, butcher twine, and aluminum foil are all things I keep handy in the kitchen.

The Pantry 100

I'm a firm believer in a well-stocked pantry. In fact, mine is probably over-stocked. As I was working on the recipes for this book, I found that I fell back on the same pantry items over and over again, and so I thought it would be good to make a list of those items. This might seem like a daunting list, but the idea isn't that you should go out and purchase all of these immediately. It's just to give you an idea of things that you might try to keep on hand to make life easier in the kitchen.

Also, this is far from a complete list of all the ingredients used in this book, but it's a fantastic start and is simply the most common one hundred ingredients that I used in these recipes. Most are nonperishable or have long shelf lives. The top one hundred are:

- All-purpose flour
- Almond extract
- Apple cider vinegar
- Baking powder
- Baking soda
- Balsamic vinegar
- Bay leaves
- Black beans (dry and/or canned)
- Black peppercorns
- Bread crumbs (regular and panko Japanese style)
- Bread flour
- Butter
- Cake flour
- Canned chipotle peppers in adobo
- Canned green chiles
- Canned tomatoes
- Capers
- Cardamom pods
- Cayenne pepper
- Chili garlic sauce
- Chili powder
- Chocolate chips (milk, semi-sweet, and dark)
- Cinnamon (ground and sticks)
- Cocoa powder
- Coconut milk
- Coffee
- Coriander
- Cornmeal
- Cornstarch
- Corn tortillas
- Cumin
- Curry powder
- Dried basil
- Dried chiles
- Dried cranberries
- Dried mushrooms
- Dried oregano
- Egg noodles
- Eggs
- Fish sauce
- Flour tortillas
- Frozen vegetables (corn and peas are my favorites)
- Garlic
- Garlic powder
- Graham crackers
- Green olives
- Ground flax seed
- Ground ginger
- Honey
- Hot sauce
- Kalamata olives
- Ketchup
- Kimchi
- Lemons
- Lentils

- ☐ Limes
- ☐ Maple syrup
- ☐ Mayonnaise
- ☐ Mustard (I like Dijon)
- ☐ Nutmeg
- ☐ Old Bay Seasoning
- ☐ Olive oil
- ☐ Paprika (regular and smoked)
- ☐ Parmesan cheese
- ☐ Pasta
- ☐ Peanut butter
- ☐ Pecans
- ☐ Pickles
- ☐ Pistachios
- ☐ Polenta
- ☐ Powdered sugar
- ☐ Red pepper flakes
- ☐ Red wine vinegar
- ☐ Rice (brown, white, long and/or short grain)
- ☐ Rice noodles
- ☐ Rice wine vinegar
- ☐ Rolled oats
- ☐ Salsa
- ☐ Salt (kosher and table)*
- ☐ Sesame seeds
- ☐ Shredded coconut
- ☐ Slivered almonds
- ☐ Soba noodles
- ☐ Soy sauce
- ☐ Sriracha chili sauce
- ☐ Stocks (vegetable and chicken—homemade is always best, but having a few store-bought boxes on hand doesn't hurt)
- ☐ Sugar (brown and white)
- ☐ Sun-dried tomatoes
- ☐ Sunflower seeds
- ☐ Tarragon vinegar
- ☐ Toasted sesame oil
- ☐ Tofu
- ☐ Tomato paste
- ☐ Tortilla chips
- ☐ Vanilla extract
- ☐ Vegetable oil
- ☐ Whole wheat flour
- ☐ Worcestershire sauce
- ☐ Yeast, active dry
- ☐ Yogurt (normal and Greek)

---

* Salt is one of the most important ingredients in your kitchen arsenal for enhancing flavor. Throughout the book I use "salt and pepper" as an ingredient, which means you should season the dish to your liking. When it makes a difference to the recipe, I specify table salt or kosher salt. In general, I prefer kosher salt for everyday cooking because it's harder to over-salt a dish with it.

Food Storage Tips

If you are going to be using leftovers effectively, it's very important that you know how to store food correctly. The difference between storing food poorly and well can be the difference between three days or six days of usage. That's money in your pocket!

As far as containers go, I recommend splurging for a nice set of glass storage containers. They keep the food airtight and are also easier to clean and don't stain. You can freeze them without issue and microwave them safely. They are more expensive but worth every penny. I've had the same set for three or four years now, and they still look like new and work great.

Here are some things to keep in mind when storing food:

- **Cool it down.** Never move very hot food into the fridge. Hot food creates condensation that will make your food spoil faster. Also, a hot container will heat up your entire fridge or freezer and cause other food to spoil faster. That said, you don't need to let the food come to room temperature before storing. Most modern fridges can handle warm food, and you don't want to leave food sitting out for hours. As a rule I always try to store food within an hour of cooking it, which is normally enough time for it to cool slightly.

- **Big pieces keep better.** Large chunks of food have a better shelf life than smaller chunks. In the salmon chapter, for example, you'll get more life out of your salmon if you can keep it in big fillets and then flake it off as needed. If you flake it first and store it, you'll probably lose a few days of your shelf life.

- **Airtight is best.** This may sound like common sense, but the more airtight you can keep most foods, the longer they will keep. This is especially important if you are freezing food, because any air will lead to freezer burn. Having good storage equipment helps, but you might also consider wrapping items in foil or plastic wrap and then storing them in airtight containers to improve storage times.

- **Use common sense.** If you open something in your fridge and it smells off or strange, don't risk it. I've tried to give guidelines in each chapter for how long each main dish can be stored, but this time could vary depending on your environment. Obviously, the sooner you can eat leftovers, the better they will be, but if something doesn't look or smell right, then use your best judgment.

I don't know about you, but reading all of this information about food and equipment makes me hungry. Let's dig into some recipes!

CHAPTER 2
ROAST CHICKEN

When I think of meals that completely embody the leftover philosophy, I think first of roast chicken. It follows all the rules: It's perfectly delicious as is, it keeps nicely for days, and you can use every bit of it to make a variety of other meals. But I've noticed that people are afraid to roast a chicken. After all, there's a whole bird of things that could go wrong.

But guess what? Even if you don't tie the bird perfectly (or at all), or don't season it evenly, you're still going to wind up with many fantastic meals. In reality, roast chicken is probably a lot more forgiving than many other dishes you make.

If you're in a pinch and don't feel like roasting a chicken, the supporting recipes in this chapter can almost all be made with any leftover shredded chicken. You could even buy a rotisserie chicken from your local deli and use that in the recipes.

Depending on the size of your family or how many other dishes you want to make, you will most likely need to roast more than one chicken. One roast chicken will easily feed a family of four or yield about half its weight in shredded chicken, which can then be used for two or three other dishes.

Simple Roast Chicken

When it comes to selecting a chicken, pick the best bird you can afford. Free-range and organic chickens not only have an ethical advantage over the factory-farmed birds but also tend to have more flavor and, in my opinion, will be healthier for you and your family. For a few extra bucks, you really can't go wrong.

Servings: 4, or 2 pounds shredded chicken | Prep Time: 10 minutes | Total Time: 90–120 minutes

1 (4-pound) chicken

1–2 tablespoons kosher salt

Olive oil

Freshly cracked pepper and salt to season

Note on Cooking Time: Depending on the number of chickens you're roasting at once, your cooking time will change. As a general rule, add 15 minutes for each extra bird you have in the oven at one time. At the end of the day, a meat thermometer is your best friend for knowing when they are done. When it comes to thermometers, I prefer a digital probe thermometer that can be left in the chicken during cooking.

1. If time permits, it's best to salt the chicken the day before you plan to cook it. For best results, rub the bird with the kosher salt and then wrap it in plastic wrap. This will result in a juicier and more flavorful finished product, though I've definitely skipped this step with fine results.

2. When you're ready to cook the chicken, preheat oven to 400°F. Whether or not you salted your chicken, rinse it under cold water and pat it dry. Drizzle with olive oil and rub salt and pepper all over the chicken. Be sure to get inside the cavity as well.

3. For a more pleasing presentation, tuck the wings under the body and tie the drumsticks together with a bit of kitchen twine so they stay snug to the body. No need to do anything fancy. Again, I've skipped this step with fine results, but if you don't tuck the wings back, they will burn.

4. Roast the chicken, breast side up, until the juices run clear and the chicken registers 170°F in the thickest part of the thigh. (In actuality, I always pull mine around 165°F because it will continue to cook after you take it out, but my lawyers say I should specify 170°F.)

5. This roasting will probably take about 90 to 100 minutes for a 4-pound bird, but I recommend using a meat thermometer to ensure that it's done. Baste the chicken with the juices and rotate the pan every 30 minutes.

6. When the chicken is done roasting, cover it loosely with foil and let it rest for 10 minutes before slicing into it.

Six Roast Chicken Variations

VARIATION	INGREDIENTS	PREPARATION
Herbed Butter Chicken	½ cup unsalted butter ¼ cup chopped parsley 1 tablespoon chopped fresh thyme 1 tablespoon chopped fresh rosemary 1 ½ tablespoons kosher salt 1 tablespoon black pepper	In a food processor, combine all ingredients and pulse until mixed well (or chop finely and mix well in a small bowl). Generously rub dried bird inside and out with mixture. Roast normally. Baste frequently with juices.
Citrus Zing Chicken	2 lemons 2 limes 1 orange 1½ tablespoons kosher salt 1 tablespoon black pepper	Zest the fruit and combine zests, salt, and pepper. Coat bird well with mixture (preferably the night before cooking). Before cooking, stuff cavity with zested lemons, orange, and limes and roast normally.
Five Spice Chicken	1½ tablespoons kosher salt 1 tablespoon black pepper 1 tablespoon vegetable oil 1 tablespoon sesame oil 1 tablespoon five spice powder 1 tablespoon honey A few inches fresh ginger, chopped 1 orange, peeled and sectioned	Whisk together salt, pepper, oils, spice powder, and honey and coat bird. Add ginger and orange pieces to bird cavity. Check bird every 20 minutes while roasting. If pan is dry add ⅓ cup water to make the glaze liquid again and baste bird. The final chicken should have a nice dark glaze on it.
Italian Pesto Chicken	1 cup fresh basil 2 cloves garlic ¼ cup pine nuts, toasted ¼ cup olive oil Juice of 1 lemon ¼ cup Parmesan cheese Pinch of salt and pepper	Combine all ingredients in a food processor and pulse until well mixed. Use just the juice from the lemon for the pesto, but add the lemon itself to the cavity of the chicken. Rub pesto over bird and roast normally.
Hot Maple Chicken	¼ cup pure maple syrup ¼ teaspoon cayenne ¼ teaspoon ground ginger Juice of 1 lemon A few inches fresh ginger, chopped Pinch of salt and pepper	Combine maple, cayenne, ground ginger, lemon juice, salt, and pepper. Add lemon and ginger pieces to chicken cavity. Rub chicken with maple mixture and roast normally, basting frequently.
Tandoori Chicken	1 cup Greek yogurt ¼ cup lemon juice 4 cloves garlic, minced 2 inches fresh ginger, minced 2 teaspoons ground cumin ½ teaspoon cayenne Pinch of salt and pepper	Combine all ingredients in a bowl and rub the chicken well with marinade. If possible, try to get marinade under the skin as well. Let marinate overnight. Wipe off excess marinade before roasting at 425°F until the chicken reaches 165–170°F.

Shred the Evidence

All the recipes in this chapter work off loosely shredded chicken from the leftovers of your roasted bird. After the chicken cools slightly, use your fingers to pick off as much of the meat as you can from the bones. It'll be a bit messy, but it doesn't take too long. Try not to include the skin or too much fat or cartilage. Shredded chicken will keep fine refrigerated in an airtight container for 5 days. If you want to store the chicken longer, keep it whole (7 days roughly), or freeze the shredded chicken and it will be fine for a few months. Use the carcass to make Roast Chicken Stock.

Trussing a Chicken

It's not entirely necessary to truss your bird, but it does help the chicken cook evenly. If you want to try trussing, this is how I do it.

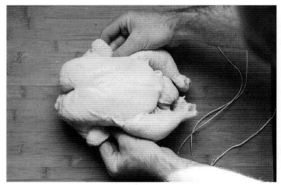

1. Whether you are trussing your chicken or not, tuck the wings back under the bird so they will not burn during roasting.

2. Start with a 2- to 3-foot piece of kitchen twine and loop it under the drumsticks, then cross the ends and bring them down through the center of the drumsticks, pulling them together snug.

3. Keeping some tension on the twine, wrap it around the bird, pulling the thighs in tight to the sides of the chicken. Your two twine ends should now be up toward the neck of the chicken. Sometimes it helps to flip the bird over during this step.

4. Tug the twine to tighten and tie it off around the neck of the chicken. Cut off any extra twine and you're ready to roast!

Roast Chicken Stock

I try to make this stock as soon as possible after roasting a chicken. I normally shred the chicken off and get this simmering as I eat dinner.

Servings: Makes 2 quarts of stock | Prep Time: 5 minutes | Total Time: 3 hours

1. After you've had a roast chicken meal and shredded the leftovers, you're going to be left with bones, small bits of meat, fat, and cartilage. Immediately toss all of these items into a large pot along with the onion, carrots, celery, peppercorns, bay leaves, garlic, parsley, and water.

2. Bring this to a simmer and cook, partially covered, for about 3 hours. Skim off any foam that accumulates as the stock simmers. Let the stock cool to room temperature, strain it, and refrigerate or freeze. You'll use some of it in the other recipes in this chapter.

3. While you don't have to make stock right after you roast the chicken, I always find it best to do right away, or I'll never find the time to get around to it.

1 carcass from roast chicken, meat removed and shredded

1 onion, quartered

2 carrots, quartered (or a handful of baby carrots)

2 stalks celery

15–20 black peppercorns

2 bay leaves

1 head garlic, split in half horizontally

A handful of parsley sprigs

Enough water to cover everything by about an inch, probably about 8–10 cups

Shredded Chicken Hash

Breakfast is no doubt the most important meal of the day, and a hearty hash with an egg is one of the tastiest meals you can wake up to!

Since you should already have shredded chicken ready, this meal is quick and simple. In fact, I frequently have it for weekday breakfasts, even though most people would consider it a "weekender." To speed things up even more, you could cube the potatoes ahead of time.

Servings: 2 | Prep Time: 5 minutes | Total Time: 20 minutes

2 tablespoons olive oil

2 medium russet potatoes, scrubbed and chopped into ½-inch cubes

Salt and pepper

4 ounces (1 cup) shredded chicken

2 large eggs

½ teaspoon smoked paprika (optional)

Hot sauce (optional)

1. In a large heavy pot or cast-iron skillet, heat oil over medium-high heat. Add potatoes and a pinch of salt. Cook potatoes until lightly browned, stirring occasionally, about 10 minutes.

2. Add shredded chicken and continue to cook until potatoes are crispy but tender on the inside, about another 5 minutes.

3. Remove hash to a plate and crack two eggs into the pan. There should be enough oil in the pan to cook the eggs, but if your pan is dry, add another drizzle of oil. Cook eggs as you like. I like mine sunny-side up!

4. Divide hash between two plates and top with eggs. I love to garnish mine with smoked paprika and hot sauce, but some people might prefer ketchup.

Greek Chicken Salad

Most chicken salads I've tried over the years have been on the bland side. Chicken isn't exactly the most flavorful thing, especially if you're using canned chicken or all breast meat, which a good percentage of chicken salad recipes use.

This recipe starts off on a better footing by using really good shredded chicken from your roast chicken, but it doesn't stop there. This salad packs in some serious flavors that make it a perfect weekday lunch. I usually make a big batch of it and then use it throughout the week for lunches and snacks.

Servings: 4 | Prep Time: 20 minutes | Total Time: 20 minutes

Mix everything together except the pitas. Stuff the salad in the pita pockets, and lunch is served! It keeps fine refrigerated for a week. Doesn't get easier than that!

Note: If you microwave your pita pockets on high for 15 seconds, they will be easier to open.

1 pound (4 cups) shredded chicken

1 cup Greek yogurt

3 cloves garlic, minced

⅓ cup diced kalamata olives

⅓ cup diced red onion

½ cup diced cucumber (English cucumber works best)

½ cup quartered grape tomatoes (optional)

½ cup crumbled feta cheese

1 tablespoon minced mint

1 tablespoon minced parsley

½ teaspoon crushed red pepper flakes (optional)

1 lemon, juice only

Salt and pepper

4 pita breads, cut in half and pulled apart ready to fill

Four Chicken Salad Variations

VARIATION	INGREDIENTS	PREPARATION
Chopped Cherry Chicken Salad	4 cups shredded chicken ⅔ cup mayonnaise 1 cup chopped dried cherries 1 cup chopped walnuts or pecans ¼ cup diced shallot 2 stalks celery, diced 2 tablespoons minced fresh tarragon or thyme 2 tablespoons apple cider vinegar Pinch of salt and pepper	Toss everything together and taste. The apple cider vinegar adds a really nice tang. You could also throw in some actual diced apple for extra crunch.
Thai Chicken Salad	1 tablespoon vegetable oil 1 tablespoon chili oil 1 stalk lemongrass 2 inches fresh ginger, peeled and minced 2 red chiles, seeded 3 cloves garlic, minced 4 cups shredded chicken 1 cup diced red onion 1 tablespoon minced fresh basil Pinch of salt and pepper Romaine lettuce Sprouts Cucumbers, chopped Limes, cut into wedges Salted peanuts Soy sauce	Add vegetable oil and chili oil to a wok or large pan over high heat. Once hot, add lemongrass, ginger, chiles, and garlic. Cook on high until the veggies are softened and aromatic. Finally, add chicken. Remove from heat and mix in onion and fresh basil. Season with salt and pepper. Serve on lettuce wraps with sprouts, cucumbers, lime wedges, peanuts, and soy sauce.
Spanish Chicken Salad	1 cup mayonnaise ½ medium onion, diced ½ cup chopped sun-dried tomatoes 3 cloves garlic, minced 1 tablespoon smoked paprika 2 tablespoons Madeira (or balsamic vinegar) 2 tablespoons olive oil ¼ cup chopped parsley 4 cups shredded chicken Pinch of salt and pepper Chopped chives, garnish	Combine mayonnaise, onion, tomatoes, garlic, paprika, Madeira, olive oil, and parsley in a food processor and pulse a few times until roughly combined. Stir into shredded chicken and season with salt and pepper. Serve as an appetizer on toasted bread garnished with fresh chives.
Waldorf Chicken Salad	4 cups shredded chicken ¾ cup mayonnaise 3 stalks celery, sliced 2 apples, peeled, seeded, and diced thin 1 cup halved red grapes ½ cup chopped walnuts 1 lemon, juice only 2 tablespoons fresh thyme Pinch of salt and pepper	Combine all ingredients and taste for seasoning. Serve over lettuce or in lettuce wraps. You can also wrap this salad in a tortilla for a great lunch option.

Chicken Tortilla Soup

This is a perfect example of a good leftover dish, because it benefits from both the shredded chicken and the chicken stock that you have already prepared.

Can you use store-bought stock? Of course. But what makes this dish excellent is that the hard work is done already, so you can make a really top-notch soup in no time.

Servings: 6–8 | Prep Time: 15 minutes | Total Time: 40 minutes

2 tablespoons olive oil

1 medium onion, diced

1 cup diced carrots

1 cup diced celery

2 cloves garlic, minced

1 teaspoon ground cumin

1 teaspoon ground coriander

2 canned chipotle peppers in adobo, minced

1 tablespoon adobo sauce

1 (14-ounce can) stewed tomatoes

6 cups chicken stock (homemade is best)

½ pound (2 heaping cups) shredded chicken

12 (6-inch) corn tortillas (half for soup and half for topping)

1 cup rice (if you use brown, which I like best, add 15 minutes onto your total time)

Salt and pepper

Garnishes

Tortilla strips

Cilantro

Sour cream

Avocado

Lime

1. In a large, heavy pot or dutch oven, add the oil over medium-high heat. Once oil is hot, add onion, carrots, and celery. Cook for a few minutes until veggies are slightly soft.

2. Add garlic, cumin, coriander, chipotle peppers, and adobo sauce. Stir and cook for 30 seconds.

3. Add stewed tomatoes. If you have whole tomatoes, mush them up roughly before adding them. I just use my (clean) hands.

4. Once tomatoes are combined, add chicken stock and bring to a simmer. Once simmering, add shredded chicken, six diced corn tortillas (these will dissolve into the soup) and rice.

5. Simmer (covered) until rice is done. If you're using brown rice, it will take 30 to 45 minutes for it to cook. White rice will take 15 to 20 minutes. Taste for salt and pepper and season.

6. **To make tortilla strips:** Slice six tortillas into strips and spread them out evenly on a baking sheet. Bake at 400°F until crispy and slightly browned, about 10 minutes.

7. When soup is done, serve with toppings of your choice. I love tortilla strips, cilantro, sour cream, avocado, and a wedge of lime.

Spicy Chicken Tostada

Piling shredded chicken mixed with a few spicy ingredients on tortillas and adding some cheese and awesome toppings is guaranteed to please. If you aren't in a tostada mood, this filling is great in all kinds of Tex-Mex variations. You can put it on nachos, wrap it in a burrito, or triple it and use it as an enchilada filling.

Servings: 2 | Prep Time: 10 minutes | Total Time: 30 minutes

3 tablespoons vegetable oil, divided

4 corn tortillas (some grocery stores carry already-fried tostadas)

½ cup chopped onions

4 ounces (1 cup) shredded chicken

1–2 minced chipotle peppers in adobo sauce

1 cup tomato sauce

1 tablespoon adobo sauce

1 (15-ounce can) black beans, drained

Salt and pepper

1 cup shredded cheddar cheese

Garnishes

Cilantro

Avocado

Sour cream

Note: If you want your cheese really melted, once tostadas are topped, toast them in a 350°F oven for 5 minutes.

1. In a small skillet, add ½ tablespoon of oil and heat over high heat. Add one corn tortilla and cook for about 90 seconds. Flip and then cook until tortilla is crispy, about another 90 seconds. Repeat process until all tortillas are fried.

2. In a separate medium-size pan, add a drizzle of oil over medium-high heat. After a few seconds, add onions and cook until translucent and soft, about 5 minutes.

3. Add shredded chicken, chipotle peppers, tomato sauce, adobo sauce, and black beans. Cook until slightly thick and warm, about 5 minutes. Taste for salt and pepper.

4. For each serving, spoon chicken mixture over two tostadas. Then top generously with grated cheese and any garnishes you like.

Creamy Chicken Pesto Pasta

You could use any number of pastas with this dish, but I think sturdy pasta like bowtie or penne works best. I included a recipe for just enough pesto, but pesto is a good leftovers dish in itself, so I encourage you to double it. You can freeze the leftover pesto until you need it.

Servings: 4 | Prep Time: 15 minutes | Total Time: 30 minutes

1. **To make pesto:** Add ingredients to a food processor and pulse until mixture forms a paste. Be sure not to overprocess it. Some texture is good.

2. Cook pasta according to package and drain. Reserve ½ cup cooking water.

3. In a large pot, add olive oil over medium-high heat. Once hot, add onions and cook until soft, about 5 minutes.

4. Add flour to pot and whisk until it forms a paste. Cook for 1 minute. Turn down heat to medium-low and slowly whisk in milk. Stir sauce frequently at this point to prevent the milk from burning. If sauce is too thick, add more milk; if it's too thin, simmer for a few minutes to thicken it.

5. Once sauce is a light gravy consistency, stir in pesto and shredded chicken. Simmer for a minute and taste for salt and pepper.

6. Stir in pasta. If sauce gets really thick, add reserved cooking liquid from the pasta. You may or may not need it. Serve immediately.

Simple Pesto

4 ounces (2 cups)
  packed fresh basil

3 cloves garlic

⅓ cup pine nuts

⅓ cup olive oil

⅓ cup Parmesan cheese

Salt and pepper

1 pound bowtie or
  penne pasta

3 tablespoons olive oil

1 onion, diced

¼ cup all-purpose flour

3 cups warm milk

½ cup pesto

8–10 ounces (about
  2 heaping cups)
  shredded chicken

Salt and pepper

Nick Nuggets

I used to have a deal with my wife, Betsy, that if she ever had a craving for a certain fast food restaurant, I'd reproduce whatever dish she was craving. Nine times out of ten, that meant I was making chicken nuggets or french fries.

Over the years, I found the best way to make fried chicken nuggets is to use shredded chicken meat with just a few other ingredients. The breading is the key part to this recipe. It's light and super-crispy. I serve these guys with a honey-mustard sauce.

Servings: 20 nuggets | Prep Time: 20 minutes | Total Time: 45 minutes

Nuggets

12 ounces (3 cups)
 shredded chicken

1 egg

2 tablespoons all-
 purpose flour

¼ cup chicken stock or
 milk

Salt and pepper

Breading

1 cup buttermilk or milk

1 egg

2 cups all-purpose flour

1 tablespoon paprika

1 teaspoon baking soda

Salt and pepper

1 quart canola or
 vegetable oil for frying

1. Chop your shredded chicken until it's in small pieces. Try to make it an even consistency, but don't worry about it if there are some bigger pieces. Also, buck the trend and use white and dark meat. It'll result in a moister nugget.

2. Combine chopped chicken with egg, flour, and chicken stock or milk to provide some moisture for the filling. Add a pinch of salt and pepper and stir well to combine.

3. Mix buttermilk (or milk) and egg together in a bowl. In a separate bowl, mix flour together with paprika, baking soda, and a pinch of salt and pepper.

4. Form balls of chicken filling about two tablespoons in size (a bit smaller than a golf ball). The filling should stick together loosely, but if it doesn't, add a few tablespoons of flour to your chicken filling until it sticks together and holds a ball shape.

5. Dip each nugget in flour mixture, then buttermilk, then again in flour, and set aside on a baking dish. Prepare all the nuggets before you start frying.

6. Heat frying oil to 350°F in a deep pan or skillet and fry nuggets until they are a nice golden brown, about 3 to 4 minutes on each side. Work in batches and don't crowd the pan.

7. Remove the nuggets to a plate lined with a paper towel and sprinkle immediately with a pinch of salt.

8. You can keep the nuggets warm in a 250°F oven on a baking sheet (no paper towel in the oven) while you fry the others.

9. Serve with your favorite dipping sauce. I like a honey-mustard sauce that's two parts Dijon mustard and one part honey.

Chicken and Dumplings

There are two things that are absolutely true:

1. Real, homemade chicken and dumplings can bring a smile to any face.

2. Real, homemade chicken and dumplings can't be made on a weekday without using leftovers.

   If you make some good stock and hang on to a few cups of shredded chicken, you'll be able to serve up a dish that normally takes hours in just a few minutes.

Servings: 4 | Prep Time: 20 minutes | Total Time: 40 minutes

4 tablespoons unsalted butter

1 medium onion, diced

2 stalks celery, diced

1 cup diced carrots

4 tablespoons all-purpose flour

3 cups chicken stock, warmed

8 ounces (2 cups) shredded chicken

Salt and pepper

Dumplings

2 cups cake flour (you can sub all-purpose flour, but your dumplings won't be as light and fluffy)

2 teaspoons baking soda

1 teaspoon kosher salt

2 tablespoons unsalted butter

¾ cup milk

1 cup frozen peas (optional)

Freshly chopped parsley, garnish

1. In a large, heavy pot with a lid or a dutch oven, add 4 tablespoons butter over medium-high heat. Once melted, add onions, celery, and carrots and cook for 5 minutes.

2. Add flour to vegetables and stir until it forms a paste. Cook for 1 minute, until flour starts to turn a light brown color.

3. Slowly stir in chicken stock. Add it in ½-cup batches so the mixture stays smooth. It should have the consistency of a light gravy. If it's too thick, add more stock. If it's too thin, simmer for a few minutes until it thickens or sprinkle in another tablespoon flour.

4. Stir in shredded chicken and season with salt and pepper. Bring dish to a simmer, then turn down heat to low.

5. In a small bowl, combine cake flour, baking soda, and salt. Melt 2 tablespoons butter and add to dry ingredients along with the milk; stir to combine. Don't overmix the dumpling batter.

6. Using a large spoon, drop heaping spoonfuls of dumpling batter into the pot. Spread them around and don't stack them. You want each dumpling to be partially submerged in liquid.

7. As soon as all of your dumplings are in, cover the pot and cook over low heat for 15 minutes. Don't open the lid!

8. Once 15 minutes have passed, add peas (if you're using them), stir, and taste for salt and pepper.

9. Serve with chopped fresh parsley and enjoy! Any leftovers can be reheated with a little milk or chicken stock.

CHAPTER 3
BLACK BEANS

My wife can be a serious jokester, which is just one of the many reasons why I love her. When I was writing this chapter, there was a period of time when we were eating black beans multiple times a day—every day.

One day, she said half-jokingly, "Be sure to include a recipe for Bean-o in that chapter you're writing." Touché, my dear.

It is true that beans have a certain reputation, and not without reason. So let's just say it: They can give you gas.

There are a few reasons for this, most of which are easily solvable. First, how you prepare the beans can have a lot to do with how you digest them. If you rinse and soak the beans well, and discard the soaking water, you should notice much less of an effect.

Second, most people aren't used to eating a lot of high-fiber veggies, and their digestive systems aren't accustomed to them. If you want beans to play nice with your system, the real secret is to actually eat more of them. You don't need to eat them at every meal or every day, but incorporating them regularly into your meals will most likely solve the problem.

If, however, you experience extreme discomfort when you eat beans, you should see your doctor, as it could be due to an allergy or some other issue.

Now that that's out of the way, let's talk about why I love beans. For starters, they are dirt cheap. You can buy a pound of dry beans for a buck. That's pretty hard to beat. Not to mention that they keep perfectly for a week once they are made.

Besides being cheap and storing well, the spicy black beans in this chapter are delicious on their own, but they can also be incorporated into a wide range of cuisines and dishes. If you can occasionally cook a big pot of beans, I think you'll be pleased with the variety of meals you can make.

Even I don't make dried beans every time I feel like having a bean dish. Canned beans are also a staple in my pantry. They are a bit more expensive but obviously way faster than the dried variety. There are two important things to remember about canned beans if you are using them in the recipes in this chapter: (1) Be sure to rinse your canned beans well under cold water before using them in a recipe, and (2) canned beans tend to be a bit softer than homemade beans, which could result in some texture differences. If you're using canned beans in something like the Black Bean Burgers recipe, you may have to add a bit more binder to get the mixture to hold together.

Spicy Black Beans

There's an easy shortcut for almost all the recipes in this chapter: canned beans. If you're pinched for time, you can buy a few cans of black beans, drain and rinse them well, and use them in all of the dishes that follow in this chapter. How's that for flexible?

But the real magic of this chapter comes when you start using dry beans. Economically, it's a no-brainer. One pound of dry beans (about $1) will cook over two pounds of finished beans, or about four cans. The cheapest I've been able to find canned black beans recently is 75 cents a pop, so you're looking at a decent savings every time you use dried beans.

Of course, the main reason I like to cook beans from scratch is so I can customize them. While they are cooking, you can toss in all kinds of peppers and other ingredients to give them some really nice flavor that you'll never get out of a canned variety.

Once they are cooked, they'll store fine in the fridge for five to seven days. You can also freeze beans after you soak them but before you finish cooking them.

Servings: Makes about 8 cups of beans | Prep Time: 15 minutes (plus soaking time) | Total Time: 90–120 minutes

Cooking Liquid

1 pound dried black beans, soaked

1 onion, halved

2 bay leaves

2 dried chiles, New Mexico or poblano

1 teaspoon dried oregano

2 cloves garlic, halved

2 tablespoons olive oil

½ large onion, diced

1 jalapeño, seeds included, diced

1 teaspoon cumin seeds

1 teaspoon red pepper flakes

1 cup cooking liquid or vegetable stock

Salt and pepper

1. Pour dried beans onto a sheet pan and quickly sort them to remove any debris or rocks.

2. Soak the beans overnight in cold water. If you don't have time to soak, add beans to a large pot and cover with 2 inches of water. Bring to a boil and cook for 2 minutes, turn off heat, cover, and let sit for 45 minutes.

3. Once your beans have soaked, rinse them well and add them to a large pot. Cover the beans with a few inches of water and add the onion, bay leaves, chiles, oregano, and garlic.

4. Bring to a simmer and cook, slightly covered, until beans are tender, probably 60 to 90 minutes. Taste the beans occasionally so you don't overcook them.

5. Drain beans, reserving some cooking liquid if you want. Pick out the cooked onion, bay leaves, peppers, and garlic cloves from the beans.

6. In a large skillet, add olive oil over medium-high heat. Once oil is hot, add onion and jalapeño. Cook for a few minutes until soft.

7. Add cumin seeds and red pepper flakes to the pan and cook for another minute.

8. Stir in cooked black beans. Add reserved cooking liquid or some warm vegetable stock to beans and stir to combine.

9. Season with salt and pepper and serve immediately, or cool and store for later.

Huevos Rancheros Cups

When you have a huge container of black beans in the fridge, Tex-Mex style dishes are some of the easiest to make and will be featured pretty heavily in this chapter. When it comes to breakfast dishes, one of my favorites is huevos rancheros. The combination of a runny egg with spicy beans, melted cheese, and salsa is a fantastic way to start the day.

It shouldn't surprise you to hear that this dish is one of my top ten breakfasts when I'm recovering from a long night out. It's an instant cure for a hangover!

Servings: 4 huevos rancheros cups | Prep Time: 5 minutes | Total Time: 30 minutes

1 cup cooked black beans

Pinch of ground cumin

2 tablespoons fresh cilantro (optional)

1 tablespoon vegetable oil

Salt and pepper

4 corn tortillas

2 ounces cheddar cheese, grated

4 large eggs

1 avocado

Salsa

1. Brush four ramekins with vegetable oil and preheat your oven to 350°F.

2. In a small bowl, mash together the black beans, cumin, cilantro, and vegetable oil, and season with salt and pepper.

3. Cover corn tortillas with a paper towel and microwave for 20 seconds so they are flexible. Press tortillas down into ramekins. Be careful not to tear the tortillas too much.

4. Divide bean mixture evenly among the four tortilla cups. Cover bean mixture with grated cheese and top each tortilla cup with an egg.

5. Bake until the whites in the eggs are set, 20 to 25 minutes. The yolks should be slightly runny.

6. Remove tortilla cups from ramekins once they cool slightly. If the tortillas stick at all, run a knife around the outside to loosen the tortillas. You can also eat the cups straight out of the ramekins, which might be easier.

7. Top huevos rancheros cups with avocado and salsa and serve immediately.

Note: If you don't have ramekins, you can bake these flat on a baking sheet. Just oil a baking sheet and slap down a few tortillas. Add some beans and cheese. Make a small well in the bean mixture for the egg to sit in and then bake for 15 to 20 minutes.

Black Bean Burgers

This is about as meaty as a veggie burger can get. Once you try this burger laced with spices and tasty black beans, you'll have a hard time going back to frozen veggie burgers. Even as a meat eater, I eat this burger every chance I can get. It's just plain delicious.

These burgers can be a bit fragile. I highly recommend cooking them in a skillet the first time you make them. If you don't have a lot of grilling experience, they might fall apart when you flip them. If they are falling apart on you, add two more tablespoons oil and flour, and another one-quarter cup bread crumbs.

Servings: 4 large burgers | Prep Time: 10 minutes | Total Time: 30 minutes

1. In a large skillet, heat a tablespoon of olive oil over medium-high heat. Add peppers, garlic, and onions to skillet and cook for a few minutes until soft. Add cumin, chili powder, and oregano to skillet and continue to cook until spices are fragrant, about another minute.

2. Add skillet mixture to a bowl with cooked black beans. Mash mixture together well. Add in egg and bread crumbs.

3. Form four even-size patties with the bean mixture. It should be wet enough to stick together, but not soupy. If necessary, add more bread crumbs or a tablespoon of oil to the mixture to give it a good consistency. If you're using canned beans for this recipe, the beans will have more liquid so you will need an extra tablespoon or two of bread crumbs. Season each patty well with salt and pepper.

4. Cook burgers either on the grill or in a large skillet (skillet is easier). Either way, cook them on high heat for 2 to 3 minutes per side. If you're using a skillet, be sure to add some oil to the pan so they don't stick.

5. Once the burgers are flipped, add grated cheese to each burger (if you're using it).

6. Serve burgers on sturdy buns with sliced avocado, cabbage slaw, and any other fixings that you want.

7. **For slaw:** Stir shredded cabbage with vinegar and salt.

1–2 tablespoons olive oil

⅓ cup diced red pepper

1 clove garlic, minced

⅓ cup diced red onion

1 teaspoon ground cumin

1 teaspoon chili powder

1 teaspoon dried oregano

2½ cups cooked black beans

1 large egg

⅔ cup bread crumbs

Salt and pepper

4 ounces (1 cup) grated cheddar cheese (optional)

1 avocado, sliced

4 sturdy hamburger buns

Quick Cabbage Slaw

2 cups shredded green or purple cabbage

¼ cup apple cider vinegar

1 teaspoon kosher salt

Quick Refried Beans

Want a good side dish for almost any Tex-Mex meal? Refried beans are about as good as it gets. Traditionally, these are made with lard and pinto beans, but there's no rule. After all, you can mash up or puree almost any bean and it will probably be delicious. For this version, I like to use butter and black beans for a nice twist on the classic. Try these in a burrito or taco. Or just eat them with a spoon!

Servings: Makes 4 cups of beans | Prep Time: 5 minutes | Total Time: 20 minutes

3 tablespoons unsalted butter

⅓ cup minced white onion

¼ fresh jalapeño pepper, diced

⅛ teaspoon cayenne pepper (optional)

3 cups cooked black beans

1 tablespoon sour cream

¼ cup chicken or vegetable stock

Salt and pepper

1. Add butter to a skillet over medium heat until melted and simmering. Add onion and jalapeño to butter and cook until veggies are soft, about 5 minutes. Add cayenne pepper and beans and cook for another minute.

2. Add bean mixture, sour cream, and stock to a blender or food processor and blend until smooth. If mixture doesn't blend well, add a bit more stock.

3. Add bean mixture back to pan and season with salt and pepper. Serve immediately!

Tex-Mex Black Bean Soup

Soup is almost a forgotten art. These days you can buy a canned or boxed version of almost any soup you want. But trust me, the flavors in a homemade version are above and beyond anything you can find in a can. And since we have a good black bean base already made, this soup only takes a few minutes to throw together.

Servings: 6 as an appetizer | Prep Time: 10 minutes | Total Time: 30 minutes

1. Heat olive oil in a large, sturdy pot (at least 4 quarts in size) over medium-high heat until oil is hot.

2. Add onion, garlic, jalapeño, cumin, chili powder, oregano, and a pinch of salt. Cook until veggies are soft, about 6 minutes.

3. Add beans, water or stock, bay leaf, and corn (if you're using it). Bring to a simmer and cook, covered, until soup starts to thicken, about 15 minutes.

4. If you prefer a smoother soup, remove bay leaf and transfer 2 to 3 cups of the soup to a blender. Process until smooth, then return to the soup pot. If you have an immersion blender, use that to blend the soup to your desired consistency.

5. Season with salt and pepper. Serve with any or all of the optional garnishes. In my experience, the more garnishes the better!

2 tablespoons olive oil

1 cup diced white or yellow onion

3 cloves garlic, minced

1 medium jalapeño pepper, seeded and minced

1½ teaspoons ground cumin

2 teaspoons chili powder

½ teaspoon dried oregano

Pinch of salt

3 cups cooked black beans

4 cups water or vegetable stock

1 bay leaf

1 cup frozen corn (optional)

Salt and pepper

Garnishes

Sliced avocado

Grated cheese

Chopped cilantro

Lime wedges

Sour cream or crema Mexicana

Tortilla chips

Crunchy Black Bean Tacos

This is a hybrid between a quesadilla and a hard-shell taco, which may sound strange. I can guarantee, though, that once you try this method of making your own hard-shell tacos, you'll have a hard time going back to the store-bought shells. When you have the method down, you can put almost anything in these for a delicious Tex-Mex dinner.

Servings: 3–4, or 8 tacos | Prep Time: 10 minutes | Total Time: 30 minutes

2 cups cooked black beans

½ cup minced red onion

2 tablespoons minced fresh cilantro

½ teaspoon ground cumin

1 teaspoon paprika

Pinch of salt

4–6 ounces (1 heaping cup) grated Pepper Jack cheese

2 tablespoons vegetable or canola oil

8 corn tortillas

Toppings
Avocado

Hot sauce

Salsa

Sour cream

Note: Corn tortillas are resilient to heat. Don't worry about burning them; they are very sturdy. Just be sure to cook tortillas on each side long enough to get them really crispy.

1. In a medium bowl, add beans along with red onion, cilantro, cumin, and paprika. Add a pinch of salt and lightly mash all the ingredients together. Grate the cheese and have it ready as well.

2. In a large, nonstick or cast-iron skillet, add the 2 tablespoons oil and heat over medium-high heat. Add one corn tortilla at a time and let each get hot in the oil for a few seconds. Then add about ¼ cup of the bean filling to one half of the tortilla. Top with a sprinkle of grated cheese. Try not to overfill the tacos, or you might have issues flipping them without losing filling.

3. Using a spatula, carefully fold the other half of the tortilla over to form a shell. Press down lightly on the tortilla so it holds its shape. If some cheese spills out, don't worry—it will get crispy and delicious.

4. As the first taco cooks, move it to the side and begin a second one. Depending on the size of your pan, you can cook two or three tacos at once. A griddle will hold even more.

5. Cook each taco until they are nicely browned and crispy, about 3 minutes per side. When flipping the taco to cook on the other side, use a spatula and flip the taco toward the fold so the filling doesn't fall out. If your pan is very dry between batches, add another drizzle of oil.

6. Place the cooked tacos in a warm oven while you finish the rest. If the tacos are very greasy, blot them with a paper towel before moving them to the oven.

7. Serve tacos with toppings like hot sauce, salsa, avocados, and sour cream.

Smoky Black Bean Salad

It could be effectively argued that this is more of a dip than a salad, but I'm calling it a salad because it's great as a side dish. It also happens to be delicious with tortillas chips. So go crazy with it. The smoky flavor in this salad comes mainly from chipotle peppers. Don't forget to add the adobo sauce that the peppers come in. It's the best part!

Servings: 4 | Prep Time: 15 minutes | Total Time: 35 minutes

1 chipotle pepper in adobo, minced

2 cups cooked black beans

1 cup corn, fresh or frozen

3 scallions, diced

1 tablespoon adobo sauce

1 avocado, diced

¼ cup minced fresh basil

¼ cup minced sun-dried tomatoes

2 tablespoons olive oil

½ teaspoon ground cumin

½ teaspoon chili powder

½ teaspoon paprika

Salt and pepper

Tortilla chips

1. Cut off the stem of the chipotle pepper (if there is one) and slice it down the middle. Scrape out any seeds and then dice the pepper very finely.

2. Add the beans to a large bowl with the corn, scallions, adobo sauce, avocado, basil, and sun-dried tomatoes. Make sure the veggies are finely diced. You don't want a big bite of sun-dried tomatoes or a mouthful of scallions.

3. Stir in olive oil, cumin, chili powder, and paprika and taste for salt and pepper.

4. Serve as a side dish or with tortilla chips.

Chorizo Enchilada Casserole

I love enchiladas as much as the next guy, but they can be a hard dish to pull off on a weeknight. This casserole solves that problem. It has all the flavors of a delicious enchilada dish but takes a fraction of the time to pull together. The secret is to not actually make enchiladas. Just throw some corn tortillas in the casserole. Works like a charm!

Servings: 4–6 (9 x 13-inch baking dish) | Prep Time: 30 minutes | Total Time: 1 hour 15 minutes

1. Preheat oven to 450°F.

2. Cook the chorizo in a medium-size pot over high heat. Brown the meat well on all sides and break it up into pieces.

3. Remove chorizo from pot and set aside. Add black beans, chicken stock, garlic, lime juice, cumin, and chili powder to pot. Season with a pinch of salt and pepper. Bring bean mixture to a simmer and mash well to form a thin paste.

4. Add 1 cup of the bean mixture to the bottom of a 9 x 13-inch baking dish.

5. Working with one tortilla at a time, dip each one in the remaining bean mixture in the pot. Let it sit in the hot bean mixture for 10 seconds to soften. Remove soaked tortilla and fold it in half and then in half a second time, making a triangle. Place it in the casserole dish.

6. Continue with all tortillas until they are completely layered in the dish. It's okay to overlap them a bit if you need to so they all fit. Then pour remaining bean mixture over the top.

7. Sprinkle chorizo on top of casserole and finish with cheese. Bake until the casserole is bubbling and brown in spots, 25 to 30 minutes.

8. Let casserole cool slightly before serving. Don't forget to top with optional garnishes!

1 pound chorizo sausage

4 cups cooked black beans

2 cups chicken stock

2 cloves garlic, minced

1 lime, juice only

½ teaspoon ground cumin

2 teaspoons chili powder

Salt and pepper

12 (6-inch) corn tortillas

4–6 ounces (2 cups) grated Pepper Jack cheese

Garnishes

Cilantro

Avocado

Hot sauce

Sour cream

CHAPTER 4
FLANK STEAK

These days it's pretty hard to get a good cut of beef for a reasonable price. Sure you can buy dollar per pound ground beef all day long, but that's pretty far from what I consider good beef. You could also spend an average weekly salary on various cuts of dry-aged steaks. While delicious, it's not exactly realistic when feeding a family. Save the dry-aged porterhouses for special occasions.

Instead, I like to use cuts of beef that most people overlook. You can usually find good-quality beef at reasonable prices if you're willing to use the less popular cuts. While there are some exotic choices like beef tongue that most Americans aren't used to eating, there's tons of starter cuts that have a steaky flavor but with a cheaper price tag.

Flank steak is a perfect example of this. This cut is typically cheaper than regular steak cuts. That said, it seems that there has been a flank steak revival lately. Some of my recipe testers for this chapter reported paying $10 per pound for flank steak in their area. The good news is that you don't have to use flank steak for these recipes if that price is out of your budget. Feel free to use any thin, flat steak cut. The cuts labeled flap steak, skirt steak, hanger steak, or flatiron steak will all work great.

As a meal, this kind of steak works well with a side of grilled veggies (like asparagus) and some roasted or grilled potatoes.

The leftovers are incredibly versatile as well. In this chapter you'll find recipes that range from Tex-Mex to Asian. The options are pretty limitless when you have a perfectly cooked flank steak in the fridge.

Grilled Flank Steak

There are three rules when cooking flank steak, and all are equally important. If you follow them, you'll wind up with a finished steak that's on par with some of the most expensive out there.

1. Cook it hot. Whether you cook the steak on a grill or in a pan (cast-iron skillet), you want to cook it as hot as possible. When I cook flank steak, I let my grill heat up on high heat for 10 minutes before I even think about putting the steak on.

2. Keep it pink. If you overcook the steak, it will start to get tough. I don't advise cooking it past medium, but medium rare is best. For medium rare the steak should only cook for 5 to 7 minutes per side or until it has an internal temperature of about 130°F.

3. Rest it. After the steak comes off the grill, cover it with foil and let it rest for 5 minutes. Then slice it against the grain.

In case you don't know, here's what "against the grain" means: When you are prepping your steak, you'll see there are fibers running the entire length of the steak. If you were to slice the steak parallel to these fibers (lengthwise), the slices would be very tough. By slicing perpendicular to them, against the grain, you're cutting all those fibers into bite-size pieces, making each bite tender.

Servings: 4–6 | Prep Time: 10 minutes | Total Time: 30 minutes

Dry rub (see Five Flavorful Dry Rubs, page 44)

1 (2-pound) flank steak

Vegetable oil

1. Pick your favorite dry rub from page 44 and liberally cover both sides of the flank steak. Use at least 2 tablespoons of rub per side. If you have time, your steak will have better flavor if you rub it, wrap it tightly in plastic wrap, and let it sit in the fridge for a few hours.

2. Heat your grill or cast-iron skillet to high heat. If you're using a grill, be sure to let it preheat for at least 10 minutes so it's very hot.

3. Right before grilling, rub about a tablespoon of oil on each side of the flank steak.

4. Grill flank steak for 5 to 7 minutes per side, depending on thickness, for a medium rare steak.

5. When the steak is ready, cover it with foil and let it rest for 5 minutes before slicing.

6. Slice the steak against the grain. Only slice as much as you need, and store the rest of the steak whole.

Note on Steak Size

Flank steak size can vary greatly. Most commonly you will find them in 2-pound sizes, although I have found them up to 4 pounds. Since the steaks are always relatively the same thickness, the total weight of the steak shouldn't affect cooking time greatly.

I always assume that a pound of flank steak will feed three people. A 4-pound steak is the perfect size for a meal on the first day and then two or three other meals out of the leftovers. If you can only find 2-pound flank steaks, it might be worth it to cook up two of them!

Five Flavorful Dry Rubs

It should go without saying that these rubs are great on all kinds of things besides steak. Try them on chicken or pork, or even lightly sprinkled on veggies like mushrooms.

VARIATION	INGREDIENTS	PREPARATION
All Purpose Rub	1 tablespoon dried oregano 1 tablespoon paprika 1 tablespoon chili powder ½ tablespoon garlic powder 1 tablespoon kosher salt 1 tablespoon black pepper	I usually times this recipe by three or four and keep it on hand in a plastic bag or small container. It's fantastic on beef or chicken. One of my favorite uses for it is dry-rubbed baked chicken wings. Simply combine all ingredients and rub.
The Five C's Rub	1 tablespoon coriander 1 tablespoon cumin seeds 2 teaspoons cardamom seeds 1 teaspoon cinnamon 3–4 cloves 1 tablespoon kosher salt 1 tablespoon sugar	It's best to use whole spices for this rub and grind them down with a spice grinder or mortar and pestle. Try not to grind them into a dust. Some texture is good. Then mix with the salt and sugar.
Coffee Spice Rub	2 tablespoons coffee beans 1 teaspoon cardamom seeds ½ teaspoon cinnamon 1½ tablespoons chili powder 1 teaspoon garlic powder 1 teaspoon paprika 1 tablespoon kosher salt 2 tablespoons sugar 1 tablespoon black pepper	Grind coffee beans and whole cardamom in a coffee grinder or mortar and pestle and then stir with other ingredients. This has some fantastic flavor and holds up well to really meaty things. It would overpower chicken or fish though. Try instead on beef or a nice meaty pork chop.
Spicy Mustard Rub	1 tablespoon mustard seeds 1 tablespoon chili powder 1 tablespoon cumin seeds 1 tablespoon garlic powder 1 teaspoon red pepper flakes 1 tablespoon kosher salt 1 tablespoon black pepper	Grind the mustard seeds and mix with other spices. If you want a less spicy variety, leave out the red pepper flakes. It's really nice on chicken as well as beef.
The Sweet Heat Rub	2 dried chipotle peppers 1 tablespoon cumin seeds 1 tablespoon brown sugar 1 tablespoon dried oregano 1 tablespoon kosher salt 1 tablespoon black pepper 1 teaspoon paprika ½ teaspoon cayenne pepper (optional)	Roast chipotle peppers at 250°F for 15 minutes. Let cool and grind into a powder with cumin seeds. Mix with other ingredients.

Sweet Potato Hash

Some type of breakfast hash is a regular rotation for me in my meal planning, and that's because you can make almost anything with potatoes (or sweet potatoes), put an egg on top of it, and it'll be great. This version is one of my favorites. The tiny amount of brown sugar completely makes the dish because it caramelizes on the potatoes as they cook.

Servings: 4 | Prep Time: 10 minutes | Total Time: 30 minutes

2 large sweet potatoes

8 ounces (2 cups) sliced flank steak

2-3 tablespoons olive oil

½ cup minced onion

2 cloves garlic, minced

1 teaspoon paprika (optional)

Salt and pepper

1 teaspoon brown sugar

Toast

Eggs (1-2 per serving)

Hot sauce

1. Peel the sweet potatoes and dice them into ½-inch cubes. Chop up the flank steak into small pieces.

2. Add olive oil to a large, heavy skillet over medium-high heat. Once hot, add the sweet potatoes. Let sweet potatoes cook until they are crispy on one side, 5 minutes or so, then stir and continue to cook until the other side is crispy.

3. After the potatoes cook for 10 minutes, add in the onions, garlic, paprika, and a pinch of salt and pepper. Continue to cook. After 15 minutes of cooking, the potatoes should be getting nicely browned, and the onions and garlic should be soft and browning slightly.

4. Stir in flank steak and continue to cook.

5. During the last minute of cooking, stir in brown sugar. The sugar should caramelize nicely on the potatoes.

6. Serve hash with toast, fried eggs, and/or hot sauce.

Steakhouse Salad

Combining steak with salad is blasphemy to some people, but with the right flavors it can be really delicious. Since you have flank steak at the ready, this salad can be made practically on a whim.

One key to making this salad really pop is the steakhouse dressing. Take the time to try it out. It takes maybe 3 minutes to whip up and will blow any store-bought dressing out of the water.

Servings: 2 | Prep Time: 15 minutes | Total Time: 15 minutes

1. **For dressing:** Combine all ingredients in a bowl or salad dressing shaker.

2. Slice flank steak thinly and prep tomatoes, pepper, and scallions.

3. Add greens to a large bowl and drizzle with dressing. You probably won't need all the dressing. It's very flavorful, so start light with it. Toss greens with dressing to coat well.

4. Plate greens, allowing excess dressing to remain in the bowl. Top with steak and vegetables. Garnish with crumbled blue cheese and serve immediately.

Steakhouse Dressing

2 tablespoons finely minced shallot

¼ cup olive oil

2 tablespoons red wine vinegar

Dash of Worcestershire sauce

Salt and pepper

Hot sauce

8 ounces sliced flank steak

1 cup cherry tomatoes, halved

1 large roasted red pepper, sliced

2 scallions, minced

4 cups various greens: arugula, spinach, etc.

½ cup crumbled blue cheese, garnish

Chopped Steak Grilled Cheese

There is nothing particularly fancy about this dish, but it's a perfect use for leftover flank steak. The key is to make sure you use sturdy bread and also chop up the steak into bite-size pieces. Dicing the steak makes it easy to take a bite of the sandwich without pulling out a huge strip of steak. For 15 minutes of work, I'm not sure if it gets any better than this.

Servings: 2 | Prep Time: 5 minutes | Total Time: 15 minutes

6 ounces flank steak

¼ red onion, sliced thinly

2 tablespoons unsalted butter

4 slices thick, sturdy bread

3–4 ounces (1 cup) grated Pepper Jack cheese

Optional Add-ins

Mustard

Crushed red pepper flakes

Sun-dried tomatoes, minced

Fresh oregano

Fresh thyme

Sautéed mushrooms

Hot sauce

1. Slice flank steak thinly and then chop it into bite-size pieces. This makes it easier to chew in sandwich form. Slice red onion as thin as possible.

2. Generously butter one side each of your four pieces of bread.

3. Place a large skillet over medium heat. To make each sandwich, place one piece of bread, butter side down, on the skillet. Quickly add a thin layer of cheese, chopped steak, more grated cheese, onions, and any other add-ins you wish. Top the sandwich with another piece of bread, butter side up.

4. Cook the sandwich on medium heat for about 3 to 4 minutes per side. If the bread is browning too quickly, turn down the heat and flip it regularly.

5. The sandwich is done when the bread is nicely browned and the cheese is completely melted.

Note on cooking grilled cheeses: There are a huge number of sandwich presses on the market that you should feel free to use to make your grilled cheese. Personally, I still prefer a hot skillet and buttered bread because it doesn't compress the sandwich. I also find that it's easier to control temperature in a skillet.

Steak and Chili Quesadilla

Quesadillas are honestly something that can be made with almost any leftover dish. They are incredibly versatile and take just a few minutes to pull together. You could easily make a quesadilla with the chicken filling from the tostada recipe (see Spicy Chicken Tostada, page 20) or the refried black beans (see Chorizo Enchilada Casserole, page 39). If a good quesadilla isn't in your meal rotation, you're missing out!

Servings: 2 | Prep Time: 10 minutes | Total Time: 20 minutes

1. Chop the steak up roughly so it's easier to chew in the quesadilla.

2. Add a drizzle of oil to a large skillet over medium-high heat. Add steak, onions, green chiles, and chili powder, and cook for a few minutes until onions are soft and the mixture is warm. Remove steak mixture from pan. Wipe pan clean with a paper towel.

3. Add another small drizzle of oil to pan and toss in a tortilla. Let heat for 15 seconds, then pile half of the steak filling on one side of the tortilla. Top with half of the cheese. Fold tortilla in half so the filling and cheese is covered.

4. Cook tortilla until cheese is melted, about 3 minutes per side. Stash in a warm oven and repeat with the other tortilla for a second quesadilla.

5. Serve immediately with optional garnishes. Slice the quesadilla with a pizza slicer.

4–6 ounces chopped flank steak

2 tablespoons vegetable or canola oil

¼ cup minced red onion

1 (4-ounce) can green chiles

½ teaspoon chili powder

2 large flour tortillas

4 ounces (1 heaping cup) grated cheese of your choice

Garnishes

Salsa

Sour cream

Avocado

Cilantro

Hot sauce

Note: If you are cooking a bunch of quesadillas, you can also make them in the oven. Cook filling according to the above instructions. Make each quesadilla and set the quesadillas on baking sheets. Bake at 350°F for 10 to 15 minutes, flipping each quesadilla halfway through.

Spicy Beef Wontons

These might seem like an advanced dish, as they do require some practice to get them formed perfectly. The good news is that you aren't selling them in a restaurant, so they don't need to be perfect! Just do your best, and they will almost certainly turn out well. They are definitely worth the work and will wow any group as a fun appetizer. Personally, Betsy and I can easily make a meal out of them along with a side salad!

Wonton wrappers need to be refrigerated; you can find them in the cold section at your grocery store.

Servings: 25 wontons | Prep Time: 30 minutes | Total Time: 45 minutes

8 ounces (about 2 cups) diced flank steak

3 scallions, minced

1–2 Serrano peppers, minced

1 tablespoon soy sauce

1 teaspoon sesame oil

Wonton wrappers

2 quarts neutral oil for frying

Soy sauce, for dipping

Chili garlic sauce, for dipping

1. Mince your steak finely so it can work as a filling. Combine steak with scallions, peppers, soy sauce, and sesame oil in a bowl.

2. Take one wonton wrapper and lay it flat on a clean, dry surface. Place 1 heaping teaspoon of filling on the wrapper.

3. Wet the edges of the wrapper with water and fold the wrapper over, corner to corner, to make a triangle. Pick up the wonton and make a crimp in the middle, then fold the two bottom ends of the triangle so that

they overlap. Add a dab of water on the two ends to hold them in place.

4. Fold the top flap down slightly to secure the wonton. Set the finished wonton on a clean plate.

5. Once all wontons are formed, fry them in oil in batches for about 5 minutes at 350°F. As always, I recommend using a deep-fry thermometer to control oil temperature.

6. Let the wontons drain on a paper towel when they come out of the fryer. Serve immediately with soy sauce or chili garlic sauce.

Vietnamese Noodle Salad

Any salad with a full cup of freshly chopped herbs in it is going to be flavorful.

When my wife and I are in the mood for something light, we love some variation of this salad. It has crunchy vegetables in it for texture and uses a light, savory Asian dressing. This salad is great at room temperature or chilled. Feel free to make it a day in advance. It keeps nicely.

Servings: 6 as an appetizer | Prep Time: 30 minutes | Total Time: 30 minutes

Asian Dressing

3 tablespoons soy sauce

1 tablespoon toasted sesame oil

1 tablespoon chili garlic sauce

1 tablespoon brown sugar

½ lime, juice only

Dash of fish sauce (optional)

8 ounces vermicelli rice noodles

Drizzle of sesame oil

1 pound flank steak, sliced thin

1 English cucumber

1–2 Serrano peppers (optional)

1 cup shredded carrots

⅓ cup minced fresh basil

⅓ cup minced fresh cilantro

⅓ cup minced fresh mint

Soy sauce, for dipping

1. Whisk all dressing ingredients in a small bowl until well combined.

2. Cook rice noodles according to package, which should involve boiling them for just a few minutes in water. Drain the noodles, rinse them with cold water to stop the cooking, and toss them with a good drizzle of sesame oil to keep them from sticking.

3. Slice steak very thinly against the grain and set it aside.

4. Peel cucumber and remove seeds with a spoon. Slice cucumber into short sticks. If you're using the Serrano peppers, dice them as well. I remove the seeds, but you can leave them in for extra heat.

5. Add cooked noodles to a large bowl. Drizzle one quarter of the dressing over the noodles.

6. Top noodles with cucumbers, peppers, carrots, basil, cilantro, and mint. Drizzle on another quarter of the dressing.

7. Add sliced steak to the salad. Pour another quarter of the dressing over the salad and serve the last of the dressing on the side.

Beef Empanadas

This is kind of a double leftover recipe. Besides using the flank steak from this chapter, you can also use the baked potatoes from the next chapter.

You might think that these need some sort of cheese or something, but traditionally empanadas don't have cheese in them. The beef, potatoes, and spices make for a hearty filling on their own.

Servings: 12 empanadas | Prep Time: 45 minutes plus dough time | Total Time: 75 minutes

Dough

2 cups whole wheat flour

2½ cups all-purpose flour

½ teaspoon table salt

⅔ cup cold water

2 large eggs

2 tablespoons white vinegar

1 cup (2 sticks) unsalted
    butter, chilled and cubed

Filling

2–3 cups diced potatoes

2 tablespoons olive oil

1 medium white onion, diced

5 cloves garlic, minced

2 teaspoons paprika

2 teaspoons chili powder

Salt and pepper

12 ounces (about 3 cups)
    minced flank steak

1 cup diced tomatoes

½ cup diced green olives

Egg Wash

1 large egg

1 tablespoon water

Soy sauce, for dipping

1. **To make dough:** Mix flours and salt together in a large bowl. Whisk water, eggs, and vinegar together in a small bowl.

2. Using your hands or a fork, mash cubed, cold butter into dry ingredients until it forms pea-size pieces. Add wet ingredients and stir until combined.

3. Turn dough out onto a floured surface and knead a few times until the dough forms a ball. Cut the dough in half and wrap each half in plastic. Refrigerate dough for at least 1 hour, but no more than a day or it will dry out.

4. **For filling:** Cut potatoes into ¼-inch cubes and boil them in salted water until soft (or cube leftover potatoes).

5. In a large skillet, add oil over medium-high heat. Add onions and garlic and cook until soft, about 5 minutes.

6. Add paprika, chili powder, and a pinch of salt and pepper. Cook until spices are fragrant. Add potatoes and stir until potatoes are warm.

7. Finally, add steak, tomatoes, and olives. Cook for another few minutes so the flavors are combined well.

8. **To assemble:** When ready to make empanadas, preheat oven to 350°F.

9. Roll out dough on a floured surface to a large rectangle (maybe 14 by 12 inches). Cut as many 6-inch circles as you

can get out of the dough. Once you have cut out as many rounds as you can, ball the leftover dough up and roll it out once more. Cut out another set of rounds. You should get six total from each dough ball.

10. Beat together the egg and water in a small bowl for the egg wash. Add a heaping ¼ cup filling to each dough round. Brush edges with egg wash. Fold dough in half so that the filling is completely enveloped in dough. Seal empanada around the edges with a fork and poke a few holes in the top.

11. Place finished empanadas on a baking sheet lined with parchment paper and bake for 30 minutes.

12. Let empanadas cool for 5 minutes before serving with soy sauce.

Note: If you don't want to make the dough from scratch, you can find premade frozen empanada dough in some supermarkets or Latin markets.

CHAPTER 5
POTATOES

The potato is almost never the star of the American plate. It's served on the side baked with a steak or served fried next to a burger. Because of this most people make only enough potatoes for a single meal. If there are four people, there are four potatoes.

This is a huge mistake.

While potatoes may not always be the star of a meal, they can definitely be the star of a meal plan! They keep really well once they are cooked and can be used to make a huge variety of dishes. With potatoes, it's possible to make everything from breakfast to appetizers to main dishes.

While some countries (like Peru) have hundreds of different varieties of potatoes, most Americans are only presented with a few. This is sad, but okay. It means there isn't a lot to fuss over. I always recommend starting by mastering the simple Russet potato. It's cheap, plentiful, and easy to work with. If you conquer that, it's pretty easy to adapt recipes for other varieties like new potatoes or even red (or purple!) potatoes.

Because Russets are widely available, I used them as the base for this basic recipe and all of the supporting recipes as well. That makes this chapter one of the most economical in the entire book. A five-pound bag of Russet potatoes will set you back a few bucks. Compared to five pounds of flank steak or salmon, this is a deal of a chapter.

So, do me—no, yourself—a favor. The next time you are making baked potatoes, just throw in a few extra. Then, if you do nothing else, later in the week make the gnocchi in this chapter. It takes almost no time as the potatoes are already cooked, and you can thank me later.

Basic Baked Potatoes

When it comes to baking potatoes, I remember my parents always wrapping them in foil and sticking them with a fork like a voodoo doll. The problem with this method is that the skin gets completely gross as the potatoes basically steam in the foil. The way to make the best baked potatoes is to ditch the foil. This can barely be called a recipe, but it's important.

Servings: Makes 5 pounds, or 12–16 potatoes | Prep Time: 5 minutes | Total Time: 65 minutes

5 pounds russet potatoes

Olive oil

Kosher salt

1. Preheat oven to 425°F.

2. Scrub potatoes well under cold water. The skins are the best part of the baked potato in my opinion, so make sure they are clean!

3. Lay the potatoes out on a baking sheet. You'll probably need two sheets.

4. Poke a few holes in each potato with a fork and drizzle olive oil all over the potatoes. Don't be stingy with it. Use at least 1 teaspoon per potato.

5. Sprinkle each potato with kosher salt. Again, use a liberal hand. I use a few teaspoons of kosher salt for 5 pounds of potatoes. A lot of it winds up on the baking sheet.

6. Bake the potatoes for about 60 minutes. If your potatoes are abnormally large or small, you can adjust the time in either direction by 10 minutes.

Stuffed Baked Potatoes

Baked potatoes aren't exactly great on their own. They are okay if you like a large hunk of starch, but most people love baked potatoes because of what you can put on them!

Since the potato is a blank slate, you can put a ton of different delicious ingredients on it. Pick a few of the items below, set up a buffet line, and let people custom-top their own potatoes. It's sure to be a big hit.

Here are a few combinations to get you started:

Bacon + Chives + Cheddar cheese + Sour cream

Butter + Pesto + Shredded chicken

Pickled jalapeños + Chili + Sweet corn

Eighteen Baked Potato Toppings

Avocado (or guacamole)	Leftover chili
Bacon	Pesto
Butter	Roasted garlic
Cheese (almost any kind)	Roasted red peppers
Chili powder	Sautéed mushrooms
Chives	Scallions
Fresh herbs, such as basil or oregano	Shredded chicken
Grilled veggies	Sour cream
Jalapeños (pickled or fresh)	Sweet corn

Fifteen-Minute Breakfast Potatoes

If you've ever tried to make breakfast potatoes from scratch, you know that it can take some time. It's also tricky to get the restaurant-style breakfast potatoes that are nice and crispy on the outside and tender on the inside. Many attempts result in undercooked potatoes or charred cubes.

The nice thing about using leftover baked potatoes is that half the battle is over. The potatoes are already cooked, so all you have to do is add some spice and crisp them up.

Servings: 2 hearty | Prep Time: 5 minutes | Total Time: 15 minutes

3 baked potatoes

3 tablespoons olive oil

1 teaspoon paprika

½ teaspoon garlic powder

½ teaspoon red pepper flakes (optional)

Salt and pepper

1. Roughly cube the potatoes, leaving the skin on.

2. Add the olive oil to a large skillet (nonstick works well) over medium-high heat. Once hot, add the potatoes.

3. Add paprika, garlic powder, and red pepper flakes (if you're using it) and cook potatoes for a few minutes without stirring. This will give them a chance to get crispy on one side.

4. Stir the potatoes after a few minutes and continue to cook, stirring occasionally, for another 6 to 8 minutes.

5. Once the potatoes are fairly crispy and browned around the edges, season with salt and pepper and serve immediately.

Smashed Potatoes

Potatoes are best, in my opinion, when they are super crispy. Since we already have cooked potatoes on hand, we don't have to worry about cooking them all the way through. All we have to do is crisp them up in a hot oven. The result is one of my absolute favorite sides.

Besides being delicious, it's also a lot of fun to smash these guys. If you have kids, give them a mallet and let them whack away!

Servings: 4 as a side | Prep Time: 5 minutes | Total Time: 30 minutes

1. Preheat oven to 400°F.

2. Leave the skins on the potatoes and cut them into sixths. If you have really large potatoes, cut them into eighths.

3. Using a kitchen mallet or really anything heavy, gently smash the potatoes until they are flat. It's okay if they fall apart.

4. Lay the smashed potatoes on a baking sheet and drizzle liberally with olive oil. Sprinkle with salt, pepper, and red pepper flakes.

5. Bake potatoes until they are very crispy, 20 to 25 minutes. Flip the potatoes once, halfway through.

6. Serve as a side with hot sauce and/or ketchup.

4 baked potatoes

¼ **cup olive oil**

Salt and pepper

½ **teaspoon red pepper flakes**

Hot sauce or ketchup, for dipping

Baked Potato Skins

Some of the recipes in this chapter require just the potato flesh without the skin (such as mashed potatoes and gnocchi). While you could simply discard the skins, that would be silly. You would be missing out on an opportunity to make one of my absolute favorite appetizers! Plus, the skins are the most nutritious part of the potato—they have lots of vitamins, minerals, and fiber.

Servings: 4 as an appetizer | Prep Time: 15 minutes | Total Time: 40 minutes

4 baked potatoes

Vegetable oil

1 cup grated cheddar cheese

Salt and pepper

2 scallions (both green and white parts), minced

Sour cream, for topping

1. Preheat oven to 450°F.

2. Slice whole potatoes into quarters and carefully scoop out flesh. Take care not to scoop through the skin; in fact, leave a small amount of potato on the skins. You don't want them to be too flimsy. If you have a hard time scooping out the cold potatoes, you can microwave them on high for 30 seconds. The heat will loosen up the flesh and make it easier to scoop.

3. Once you have removed most of the flesh, place potato skins, skin side up, on a baking sheet and brush with vegetable oil. Bake for 10 minutes. Remove the sheet from the oven and flip the skins over.

4. Divide grated cheese between potato skins. Season with a pinch of salt and pepper.

5. Return potato skins to the oven and bake until the cheese is well melted and the skins are crispy, 8 to 10 more minutes.

6. Top with diced scallions and serve immediately with sour cream.

Three Potato Skin Variations

Italian-Style Skins—Spoon a tablespoon of tomato sauce into the bottom of each potato skin after the first "skin side up" bake. Top with a sliver of fresh mozzarella. When they come out of the oven after the final bake, top with fresh basil.

Jalapeño Popper Skins—Mince up a whole jalapeño. After you flip the skins, add a pinch of fresh jalapeño to each skin. Top with cheddar cheese and return to the oven to finish cooking.

Breakfast Skins—Leave skins in halves instead of quarters. Whisk two eggs in a bowl with 2 tablespoons cream. When you flip the skins, divide uncooked egg mixture between the potatoes and sprinkle with grated cheese. Bake until eggs are set, about 15 minutes.

Cheesy Mashed Potatoes

If I had to guess what the majority of potatoes are used for in the United States, I'd first guess french fries, obviously, but I'd guess mashed potatoes second. People eat them with pretty much everything, and with good reason.

Since your potatoes are already cooked, mashed potatoes is just a matter of ditching the skins (or, better yet, making potato skins out of them). After you have the flesh out, it takes just a few minutes to make some really good, homemade mashed potatoes.

If you want, you can actually leave the skins on for a heartier and healthier batch of mashed potatoes.

Servings: 4 as a side | Prep Time: 5 minutes | Total Time: 15 minutes

1 pound (about 3 cups) potato flesh

2 tablespoons butter

½ cup milk

2 cloves garlic, minced

¾ cups grated cheddar cheese

Salt and pepper

Fresh minced chives, garnish

1. Add potatoes to a medium pot with butter, milk, and minced garlic. Place on the stove over medium-low heat.

2. As potatoes heat up, mash with a potato masher to incorporate the butter and milk. Continue to mash until the potatoes are an even consistency and steaming hot.

3. Add grated cheese and stir until melted.

4. Season with salt, pepper, and chives and serve immediately.

Note: If you want a super-smooth mashed potato mixture, then use a hand mixer to blend the potatoes once they are warm. Blend them before you add the cheese. You might need to add a bit more milk to get them really creamy.

Grilled Herbed Potatoes

Grilled potatoes, like breakfast potatoes, are hard to get both crispy on the outside and soft on the inside. Again, though, the nice part about having already baked potatoes is that we don't have to worry one bit about the interior. We know they are cooked, soft, and delicious. To get a really crispy crust on the potato then, we can just fire up the grill as hot as it will go and have a delicious side dish in minutes.

Servings: 4 as a side | Prep Time: 5 minutes | Total Time: 20 minutes

1. Slice baked potatoes in half lengthwise. Preheat your grill to high heat.

2. In a small bowl, mix together the oil, oregano, red pepper flakes, salt and pepper, and chives.

3. Lay potatoes out on a large tray and liberally spoon oil mixture all over the sliced side of potatoes. Let rest for a few minutes.

4. Grill the potatoes, sliced side down, for 4 to 5 minutes. Flip the potatoes and grill them for another 5 minutes on the skin side.

5. Once the potatoes come off the grill, give them a squeeze of fresh lemon juice and serve immediately.

4 baked potatoes

¼ cup olive oil

2 teaspoons dried oregano

½–1 teaspoon red pepper flakes

1 teaspoon kosher salt

1 teaspoon black pepper

2 tablespoons minced fresh chives

Squeeze of fresh lemon juice

Baked Mashed Potato Dip

Warning: This is not a diet recipe.

This is one of those recipes that you make for a lazy Sunday watching football with friends. While the recipe itself is pretty simple, you could top this dip with almost anything that you could put on a baked potato (see Eighteen Baked Potato Toppings, page 61 for some good ideas).

Servings: 6 (8 x 8-inch baking dish) | Prep Time: 15 minutes | Total Time: 45 minutes

1. Preheat oven to 350°F.

2. Slice potatoes in half and scoop out flesh. Get as much of the flesh as you can.

3. Add potatoes to a microwave-safe dish, cover, and microwave on high for 2 minutes to warm them up. They will blend better when they are hot.

4. If you're using bacon, cook it in a large skillet over medium heat until crispy. Let the bacon cool on a few paper towels and then crumble into bits. Set aside.

5. Add potatoes to a large bowl and mix with cream (or milk) and cream cheese. Use a hand mixer to whip potatoes until they are very smooth.

6. Add the scallions (whites only), garlic, and cayenne pepper to the mashed potatoes and mix until smooth and creamy. Taste potatoes and season with salt and pepper.

7. Butter an 8 x 8-inch baking dish and pour in the mashed potato mixture. Cover with grated cheese and top with diced cooked bacon. Bake for 30 minutes.

8. Garnish dish with scallion greens and serve with pita or tortilla chips.

5 baked potatoes

½ pound bacon (optional)

1 cup heavy cream or milk

8 ounces cream cheese

6 scallions, minced and separated (whites and greens)

4 cloves garlic, minced

½ teaspoon cayenne pepper (optional)

Salt and pepper

Butter (for baking dish)

1 cup grated cheddar cheese

Tortilla or pita chips, for serving

Note: If it's not creamy enough, add more milk or cream. Remember that it's supposed to be a dip.

Curried Double Baked Potatoes

When it comes to saving time, double baked potatoes don't really make sense. You are basically cooking the same thing twice, so it's not uncommon for it to take two hours to make a double baked potato from scratch. We can cut that down pretty substantially by using our leftover potatoes.

The curried paste for these is really delicious, but if it's not your style, the potatoes are good on their own as well. With the curry paste, though, this is one of my favorite recipes in this book.

Servings: 4 | Prep Time: 15 minutes | Total Time: 35 minutes

Curried Spice Paste

3 cloves garlic, mashed

2 inches fresh ginger, peeled

2 tablespoons curry powder

1 tablespoon paprika

½ teaspoon ground cumin

1 teaspoon kosher salt

⅔ cup Greek yogurt

4 teaspoons olive oil

½ lemon, juice only

Potatoes

4 large potatoes

1½ cups grated cheddar cheese

4 tablespoons unsalted butter

2 tablespoons minced cilantro

2 scallions, chopped

1–2 Serrano peppers, seeded and minced

Salt and pepper

1. Preheat oven to 350°F.

2. **To make paste:** Add garlic, ginger, curry powder, paprika, cumin, and salt to a food processor and pulse until well combined.

3. Stir in yogurt, oil, and lemon juice. It should be a very strong paste that's almost too strong to eat on its own.

4. **To prepare potatoes:** Scoop out flesh from four large potatoes. Be careful not to break through potato skins, since you will be refilling them. Microwave potato flesh on high for 90 seconds.

5. Mash potatoes with cheese, butter, cilantro, scallions, peppers, and salt and pepper. Mix thoroughly so ingredients are very well combined.

6. Lay out potato shells on a baking sheet and spoon filling back into them. You should be able to fit most of it. It's okay if the potatoes are overflowing a bit.

7. Slather each stuffed potato half with a good layer of the spice paste.

8. Bake for 25 minutes. Let cool briefly before serving.

Weeknight Gnocchi

Gnocchi is one of those meals that I think most people reserve for ordering in a restaurant. This is great news for restaurants all over the world because they can charge $15 for what is probably 50 cents worth of ingredients. Restaurants can get away with charging this much because people are intimidated by the little potato dumplings. There is no need to be intimidated!

The thing that takes the longest when it comes to gnocchi is cooking the potatoes, but guess what? That's done. So a meal that might normally be made for a Sunday dinner can be made on a Wednesday. Besides a basic gnocchi recipe, I've included two of my favorite sauces.

Servings: 4 | Prep Time: 25 minutes | Total Time: 35 minutes

1 pound potato flesh (about 3 large potatoes)

1 large egg yolk

7 ounces (about 1½ cups) all-purpose flour

Pinch of kosher salt

Basic Red Sauce

3 tablespoons olive oil

1 small sweet onion, minced

2 cloves garlic, minced

1 (28-ounce) can diced tomatoes

1 tablespoon lemon juice

1 teaspoon red pepper flakes (optional)

Salt and pepper

Parmesan cheese, grated, garnish

Freshly minced basil, garnish

Butter Sage Sauce

½ cup (1 stick) unsalted butter

6–8 fresh sage leaves

2 tablespoons gnocchi cooking water

Parmesan cheese, grated, garnish

Pinch of salt

1. Scoop flesh out of potatoes until you have 1 pound of potatoes. This is a pretty exacting recipe, so it is best to weigh both the potatoes and the flour. If you can't weigh it, then assume it's about 4 loosely packed cups of potatoes and 1½ cups of flour. Microwave potatoes for 60 seconds on high to heat them up.

2. Using a fork or a ricer, mash potatoes lightly. It's okay to have some lumps, but the smoother the better.

3. Add egg yolk, flour, and a pinch of salt, and combine well. Use your hands to knead the dough lightly in the bowl a few times until it comes together. It should be a light, fluffy dough that isn't sticky at all. If it is sticky, add more flour by the tablespoon.

4. Divide dough into fourths and roll each fourth out on a floured surface. Use a knife or dough scraper to chop up gnocchi into 1-inch dumplings.

5. Roll the back of a fork over each dumpling.

6. Lightly dust finished gnocchi with flour.

7. Shape all gnocchi before cooking them. Boil in salted water in a large pot until they float, about 90 seconds.

8. Remove gnocchi from water with a slotted spoon and serve immediately with desired sauce.

9. **To make red sauce:** Add oil to a large saucepan over medium heat. Add onions and garlic and cook for a few minutes. Add tomatoes, lemon juice, and red pepper flakes and continue to cook down for 10 minutes. Season with salt and pepper. Garnish with Parmesan cheese and basil.

10. **To make butter sage sauce:** Add butter to a large saucepan over medium heat. Cook until butter starts to take on some color, about 3 minutes. Add fresh sage leaves—you can roughly rip them up—and gnocchi cooking water. Cook for another minute and then add gnocchi straight to the sauce.

Spinach Potato Casserole

This is a very different flavor profile from the baked potato dip recipe, although it has a similar mashed potato base. It's almost a meal in a dish frankly. You have your veggies, carbs, and protein all stacked together, which always makes for a good casserole in my opinion. One hint: Don't skimp on the spinach. Use full adult spinach and use a lot of it. It cooks down substantially and can get lost in the dish if you don't use enough.

Servings: 6–8 (2½-quart or 9 x 13-inch casserole dish) | Prep Time: 30 minutes | Total Time: 1 hour

5 cups baked potatoes (about 3 or 4 medium-size potatoes)

⅔ cup heavy cream

4 tablespoons unsalted butter

Salt and pepper

½ teaspoon red pepper flakes

8 ounces (5–6 packed cups) spinach

Olive oil

2 cups (about 4 ounces) grated mozzarella or cheddar cheese

8 ounces Italian sausage (spicy is best)

1 medium white onion, sliced

1 clove garlic, minced

1 teaspoon fresh rosemary

1. Preheat oven to 350°F.

2. Peel baked potatoes and cut them into ½-inch cubes. Microwave on high for 3 minutes to heat them up.

3. Mash potatoes with cream and butter. Season with a pinch of salt and pepper and red pepper flakes.

4. Rinse spinach well (don't worry about drying it) and roughly chop. In a large skillet, add about a tablespoon of olive oil over medium heat. Once hot, add the spinach and season with a pinch of salt. Cook until spinach is wilted, just a few minutes. Stir wilted spinach and any liquid into the mashed potatoes along with the grated cheese.

5. Add another drizzle of oil into the skillet and add sausage removed from casing. Turn heat up to medium-high and let sausage brown nicely for 6 to 7 minutes. Add sliced onions and let them cook down.

6. When sausage is browned and onions are starting to brown, add minced garlic along with rosemary and kill the heat.

7. Butter or oil a large 2½-quart or 13 x 9-inch casserole dish. Spread in mashed potato mixture and top with the sausage and onion mixture.

8. Bake the casserole until the potatoes are browned around the edges and the cheese is bubbling, about 20 minutes. Let cool briefly before serving.

Potato Pizza

Honestly, almost anything can be good on a pizza. But potatoes are one of the most underrated toppings in my opinion. For this version I went the rustic route and left the potatoes with the skin on, just roughly cubing them. If you want to change it up a bit, you can mash the potatoes and use them in place of a red sauce.

I use my standard pizza dough recipe (at right), but feel free to use store-bought dough.

Servings: 4 (2 pizzas) | Prep Time: 10 minutes (plus dough time if you make homemade) | Total Time: 30 minutes

Nick's Pizza Sauce (makes 3 cups)

1 can (15 ounces) tomato sauce

½ cup water

2 tablespoons olive oil

2 tablespoons lemon juice

1 tablespoon garlic powder

1 teaspoon dried oregano

2 teaspoons dried parsley

Salt and pepper

Red pepper flakes (optional)

2 (8-ounce) pizza dough balls

Cornmeal or flour, for dusting

1 cup pizza sauce (more if you like it saucy)

14–16 ounces mozzarella cheese, grated

1 large baked potato, diced

1 cup fresh or frozen sweet corn

1 Serrano pepper, diced

Salt and pepper

Olive oil (optional)

1 handful fresh basil, minced

1. **To make the pizza sauce:** Combine everything in a bowl and let sit for a few minutes.

2. **To make the pizza:** Preheat oven to 500°F.

3. Place a pizza stone in the oven and allow it to heat up for at least 20 minutes before baking pizza to make sure it's very hot.

4. Let dough come to room temperature and then roll it out thinly on a lightly floured surface. The dough should roll out to about 10 to 12 inches in diameter.

5. Lay dough onto a pizza peel, lightly dusted with cornmeal or flour.

6. Add a light coating of sauce to dough. Then add cheese, potatoes, corn, and peppers. Season the pizza well with salt and pepper. Optionally, you can toss the diced potatoes with a tablespoon of olive oil before adding them to the pizza, so they will crisp better. They shouldn't be super oily though.

7. Slide the pizza onto the preheated pizza stone and bake for 12 minutes.

8. When the pizza comes out of the oven, top with fresh basil. Slice and serve immediately!

Napoletana Pizza Dough

This pizza dough recipe is pretty exacting, so it is best to weigh the flour. If you can't weigh it, then use about 5 cups.

Servings: 5 (8-ounce) balls (enough for 5 pizzas) | Prep Time: 20 minutes | Total Time: 5 hours

1. Combine salt, yeast, and water in a mixing bowl. Stir and let sit for 5 minutes to make sure yeast is active (it should foam).

2. Stir in flour and mix until the dough forms a loose ball. Let rest for 5 minutes and then continue to mix. You can either mix with a stand mixer (dough hook on low) or with your hands. If you use your hands, dip one in water and vigorously work the dough until it's soft but not sticky.

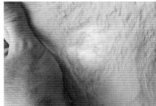

1 tablespoon kosher salt

1 teaspoon active dry yeast

2 cups room temperature water

22½ ounces (about 5 cups) bread flour

1 tablespoon olive oil

3. When dough is smooth and soft (about 8 minutes of mixing or kneading), divide dough into five balls and coat with olive oil. Let the dough sit at room temperature for 30 minutes, then store in a large plastic bag in the fridge for at least 4 hours, or overnight. Remove dough at least 1 hour before making pizza.

CHAPTER 6
TOMATO SAUCE

Jarred spaghetti sauce is one of my least favorite inventions of the century. I get that it's quick and sometimes necessary, but if you stick a jarred pasta sauce next to a homemade version (even a quick homemade version), it's not even close. The homemade version is substantially better.

Most of the flavor from jarred sauces, regardless of what they say on the labels, comes from salt. Just lots and lots of salt. But when you make sauce yourself, you'll find that the taste is a lot more complex. It'll have a fresh tomato flavor, and whatever herbs you choose to put in it will really pop.

I would like to say that I have memories of watching my grandma stir marinara sauce for hours, the smells of basil and fresh tomatoes floating through the house. But that's just not how I was raised. I honestly didn't discover real marinara sauce until I was well out of college, and then I softly whispered to the sauce: "Where have you been all my life?"

Of course, there are various degrees of marinara sauce. There are some versions that take almost no time to cook and some that take hours. There are versions that use fresh tomatoes and others that use canned tomatoes. There are some that are herb-packed and some that are bare bones.

I'll give you the outlines for all of these variations in this chapter and then a handful of recipes you can use with your leftover sauce. None of the sauce recipes in this chapter have actually been tested for canning. For a tomato sauce to be safe to can, it needs to have a very specific pH level. But that's okay. Marinara keeps fine in the fridge for at least a week, and it also freezes really well, so there isn't a huge need to can it unless you are making a gigantic batch.

This sauce can be as simple or as complicated as you want to make it, but whatever you do, just make it.

Slow-Cooked Marinara Sauce

This is where it all starts. A large pot of tomatoes simmering with herbs and onions on the stovetop is perhaps the iconic image of Italian cooking.

For this recipe, don't even try to use fresh tomatoes unless you can find very fresh, in-season tomatoes. Using bland winter tomatoes will leave you with a lackluster sauce. If you're in doubt, just use good canned tomatoes. They work really well. If you do find yourself with perfect, fresh tomatoes, see "Working with Fresh Tomatoes" at right for advice on preparing them for your sauce.

Servings: Makes 8–9 cups of sauce | Prep Time: 10 minutes (30 if using fresh tomatoes) | Total Time: 1 hour 30 minutes (at least 2 hours with fresh)

2 medium white onions

3–4 cloves garlic

3 tablespoons olive oil

½ cup red wine

5 pounds fresh tomatoes or 3 (28-ounce) cans whole tomatoes

1 tablespoon dried basil

1 tablespoon dried oregano

1 teaspoon dried marjoram (optional)

1 teaspoon red pepper flakes (optional)

Salt and pepper

Garnishes for Pasta

Parmesan cheese

Fresh basil

Pine nuts

1. Dice onions and mince garlic. Add oil to a large, heavy pot over medium-low heat. Add onions and garlic and cook until transparent, about 5 minutes. You don't want the vegetables to brown.

2. Add red wine to pan and cook for another minute to deglaze the pan. Add tomatoes along with any juice from the tomatoes. Bring to a simmer over medium heat. Add basil, oregano, and optional herbs to the sauce, stir, and continue to cook.

3. Let the sauce simmer, partially covered, until the tomatoes break down almost completely. This will take over an hour. You can use a potato masher to help break down the tomatoes.

4. If at any point the sauce looks too thick, add ½ cup water to the sauce and continue to cook down. Keep your heat on low to medium so the sauce doesn't burn.

5. When the tomatoes are mostly broken down and the sauce is nice and thick, it's done. Taste for salt and pepper. It'll probably need a good pinch of both. If you prefer a smoother sauce, feel free to pulse in a blender or food processor until smooth.

Working with Fresh Tomatoes

Fresh tomatoes will add at least an hour onto your total cooking time for a marinara sauce, but your sauce will have a slightly fresher taste. It's not worth it, though, unless you can find very good, fresh tomatoes. I prefer to use Roma tomatoes when I make it.

To prepare the tomatoes, start by cutting a small X in the bottom of the tomato with a sharp knife. Dunk the tomatoes in boiling water for about 30 to 45 seconds, then remove the tomatoes with a slotted spoon and let them cool briefly.

Using your hands, peel off the tomato skins. Assuming you have ripe tomatoes, they should slip out of their skins without too much trouble. Use your hands to roughly rip apart the tomatoes, saving the juices. Add the dissected tomatoes to a large bowl. After all your tomatoes have been juiced, add the juice (being sure to strain it first to remove seeds) back in with the tomatoes. It's okay if a few seeds are in the mix, but try to get rid of most of them, as they will never cook down.

Use the fresh tomatoes and juice for the Slow-Cooked Marinara Sauce recipe.

Cheater's Marinara Sauce

It's not always the case that I have two hours to simmer a tomato sauce into something delicious. Sometimes I'm willing to sacrifice a bit of flavor in the name of expediency. This is the sauce I make in these moments of sacrifice. It's not quite as deeply flavorful as the slow-cooked variety, but it's still better than most jarred sauces.

The nice thing about this recipe is that it takes almost exactly as long to make as the pasta, so there's really no reason not to make it.

Servings: Makes 3 cups | Prep Time: 5 minutes | Total Time: 15–20 minutes

1 tablespoon olive oil

½ onion, diced

1 (28-ounce) can diced tomatoes

1 teaspoon garlic powder

1 teaspoon dried oregano

Pinch of red pepper flakes (optional)

Pinch of salt and pepper

1. Add olive oil to a medium pan over medium-high heat. Once hot, add onions and cook for 1 to 2 minutes.

2. Add diced tomatoes along with garlic powder, oregano, red pepper flakes (if you're using it), and salt and pepper. Bring to a simmer and cook over medium-high heat, stirring occasionally, for about 10 to 15 minutes. Mash the tomatoes lightly with a spoon or fork as sauce cooks to help speed up the process.

3. When sauce is thick and cooked down slightly, serve over warm pasta and garnish with Parmesan cheese and/or fresh basil. Optionally, you can also add pasta straight from the water to the sauce and toss to mix together.

4. Store the rest of the sauce for the other recipes in this chapter!

Eggs in Purgatory Casserole

There is a classic dish that consists of a soft-poached egg in tomato sauce, served as a hearty soup. You can easily make that with marinara sauce on hand. If you want to make the classic variation of this dish, be sure to thin out the sauce a bit with some stock or water.

I prefer to make this dish for breakfast as a kind of casserole. It's much easier to prepare and, I think, more impressive.

Servings: 4 | Prep Time: 10 minutes | Total Time: 35–40 minutes

1. Preheat oven to 350°F.

2. Lightly butter a 9 x 13-inch or 2½-quart baking dish. Line the inside rim of the dish with bread slices, cut about ¼ inch thick. It's okay if they overlap a bit.

3. Mix marinara sauce with water and reheat. If it's very thick, add ½ cup extra water to the sauce. You can reheat it in the microwave or on the stovetop.

4. Pour hot marinara sauce in bottom of casserole dish. Crack eight eggs into the sauce. Top with a drizzle of olive oil, chopped fresh thyme or oregano, and a sprinkle of salt and pepper.

5. Bake dish until egg whites are set but yolks are still runny, 25 to 30 minutes. For firm yolks, bake for another 5 to 10 minutes.

Butter, for casserole dish

Crusty bread, sliced

3 cups marinara sauce plus 1 cup water

8 large eggs

Olive oil

Pinch of fresh thyme or oregano

Salt and pepper

Note: This recipe doesn't keep well. It's meant to be served immediately out of the oven. Luckily, it is easily halved. Just use an 8 x 8-inch baking dish instead of the larger version and reduce the baking time by 5 minutes.

Classic Eggs in Purgatory

The classic version of this dish is very simple to make and works great as a weeknight meal for one or two.

1. Bring a few cups of marinara sauce to a simmer with a cup of vegetable stock to thin it out slightly.

2. Once it is simmering, crack a few eggs directly into the sauce and turn down the heat to low. Let the eggs lightly poach in the sauce for 3 minutes (the yolks should still be runny).

3. Serve the eggs and sauce in bowls with a drizzle of olive oil, salt and pepper, and a loaf of crusty bread.

Cheesy Tomato Grits

If you're in Florence, it's called polenta. If you're in Alabama, it's called grits. In reality, they are basically the same thing—that is to say, ground-up corn that's been slowly simmered. Corn and tomatoes pair well together, so simmering the grits in a diluted marinara sauce is a great way to give them some serious flavor. It's hard for me to recommend grits without cheese, so throw some of that in also!

Servings: 4 as a side | Prep Time: 5 minutes | Total Time: 30 minutes

2 cups water

1 cup milk

2 tablespoons unsalted butter

1 cup marinara sauce

1 cup coarse grits

Salt and pepper

1 cup grated cheddar cheese

1. Add water, milk, butter, and marinara to a large pot over medium heat. Bring to a simmer.

2. Once liquid is simmering, whisk in grits in a slow stream. Whisk constantly to make sure the grits don't clump together. Whisk mixture constantly over low heat until it thickens substantially. It should take 15 to 20 minutes to thicken.

3. Season the grits with salt and pepper and stir in the grated cheese. Continue to stir until cheese is melted. Serve immediately.

Polenta Squares

To keep things clear-cut, I like to call the liquid version of this dish grits and the solidified version polenta. So if you have leftover grits, you can easily make polenta. Just pour the warm leftover grits out onto a baking sheet lined with parchment paper. Let them sit at room temperature until cool, and they will harden into a single block.

Cut the block into squares and store them in the fridge until needed. When you want to serve the polenta, reheat by frying it in a bit of butter until the outside is crispy and slightly browned.

Open-Faced Italian Sandwiches

This sandwich will steal your heart. Never again will you feel the need to go out to some corner shop to get a good, hot Italian sub. Once you have a solid base of marinara sauce, the sandwich basically builds itself.

As you can see from the list below, the options are pretty endless when it comes to toppings. Sometimes I like a simple variation that I call The Margherita Sandwich, which is just sauce and fresh mozzarella, finished with fresh basil. But you can go crazy with your own version.

For an appetizer option, make a full loaf and chop it into sticks.

Servings: 2 | Prep Time: 5 minutes | Total Time: 15 minutes

1. Preheat oven to 500°F.

2. Cut loaf of bread in half horizontally. Top each half with a good smear of marinara sauce. Add sliced cheese on top of marinara sauce, along with any other toppings. Season with salt and pepper.

3. Bake sandwich until bread is toasted and cheese is melted and bubbly, 8 to 10 minutes. Let cool slightly before serving.

1 loaf rustic Italian bread
¾ cup marinara sauce
8 ounces sliced mozzarella cheese
Drizzle of olive oil
Salt and pepper

Eighteen Italian Sandwich Toppings

Anchovies

Buffalo mozzarella

Capers

Fresh herbs (basil, thyme, oregano)

Fresh tomatoes

Kalamata olives

Marinated artichokes

Marinated garlic

Marinated mushrooms

Pancetta

Parmesan cheese

Pepperoni

Pickled jalapeños

Red onions

Roasted red peppers

Salami

Sun-dried tomatoes

Sweet peppers

Tomato Cream Soup

There's a fine line between soup and sauce, which is great news for us. Assuming you have some delicious sauce made, it just takes a few small tweaks and a blender to turn it into a hearty soup! Making this soup is basically as fast as opening a can and warming it up, so there's really no reason not to try it out if you are a soup fan and have some good marinara on hand.

Servings: 4 as an appetizer | Prep Time: 5 minutes | Total Time: 15 minutes

4 cups marinara sauce

2 cups vegetable or chicken stock

1 cup heavy cream

Salt and pepper

Fresh basil

Crusty bread

1. Add marinara sauce to a blender or food processor and pulse until mostly smooth. Some small chunks are okay.

2. Add sauce to a pot over medium heat along with stock. Bring to a simmer and cook for a few minutes. Stir in cream and continue to simmer for another 2 to 3 minutes. Be careful to stir often or it will burn.

3. Season the soup with salt and pepper. Serve with fresh basil and lots of crusty bread.

Fire and Smoke Pizza

I first had a pizza like this when I was living in Washington, DC, at a popular pizza joint in Chinatown called Matchbox. They really do make great pies, and even today, this is my favorite. The intense heat from the chipotle pizza sauce pairs perfectly with the smokiness from the Gouda. I'm not sure about the actual recipe they use. This is just my version.

Servings: Makes 2 pizzas | Prep Time: 15 minutes (plus dough time if you make homemade) | Total Time: 30 minutes

1. **To make the sauce:** In a food processor, pulse together marinara sauce, chipotle peppers (I even leave the seeds in), and adobo sauce. It should be very spicy on its own. Remember that it won't be as potent on the pizza because of all the toppings.

2. **For the pizza:** Let dough come to room temperature and then roll it out thinly on a lightly floured surface. The dough should roll out to be about 10 to 12 inches in diameter.

3. Preheat oven to 500°F. If you have a pizza stone, preheat it in the oven for 20 minutes.

4. Add dough to a pizza peel (or back of a sheet pan) lightly dusted with cornmeal or flour. Add a light coating of chipotle marinara sauce to dough. Then add cheeses and vegetable toppings.

5. Carefully slide pizza onto the preheated pizza stone and bake for 10 to 12 minutes.

6. When pizza comes out of the oven, let it cool for a minute. Slice and serve!

Chipotle Pizza Sauce (makes 1 cup)

1 cup marinara sauce

3–4 chipotle peppers, in adobo sauce

2–3 tablespoons adobo sauce (from peppers)

2 (8-ounce) pizza dough balls

1 cup chipotle pizza sauce (or more if you like it saucy)

8 ounces mozzarella cheese, grated

6 ounces smoked Gouda, grated

1 red onion, sliced thin

2 roasted red peppers, sliced thin

Note: For homemade pizza dough, check out Napoletana Pizza Dough, page 77.

Mozzarella Ball Baked Pasta

As a food writer, I have an obligation to include at least one rock solid baked pasta dish in a chapter dedicated to marinara sauce. This recipe creates exponential returns on your leftover sauce. It makes a deep 9 x 13-inch baking dish of delicious baked pasta, so you'll almost certainly have leftovers from this meal as well.

Servings: 6 (9 x 13-inch baking dish) | Prep Time: 25 minutes | Total Time: 1 hour

1 pound pasta (I like chiocciole, penne, or ziti)

3 cups marinara sauce

2 tablespoons olive oil

1 pound mini mozzarella cheese balls

Salt and pepper

1 teaspoon red pepper flakes (optional)

1 tablespoon unsalted butter (for dish)

½ cup grated Parmesan cheese

1 cup Italian bread crumbs

1. Cook pasta in heavily salted water according to package until it's al dente. Be careful not to overcook the pasta or your baked dish will be soggy. You can use a wide range of pastas for this dish. I recommend something tubular like ziti, chiocciole, or penne.

2. Heat marinara sauce over medium heat on the stovetop until it's lightly simmering.

3. Preheat oven to 350°F.

4. Drain pasta and drizzle with olive oil, then toss with marinara sauce and mozzarella balls. Season pasta with a pinch of salt, pepper, and red pepper flakes (if you're using them).

5. Add pasta mixture to a lightly buttered 9 x 13-inch baking dish. Top with Parmesan cheese and bread crumbs.

6. Bake dish until cheese is melted and the pasta on the edges is slightly browned, about 30 minutes. Let dish cool slightly before serving.

Note: My favorite part about baked pasta dishes is that the outside edges get really crispy. If you want your pasta extra crispy, bake it for an extra 10 minutes or so.

Veggie Lasagna

Okay, so lasagna is technically just another baked pasta dish, but I consider it a different beast, especially when you layer in delicious veggies that have been sliced thin to mimic the lasagna noodles. In the scheme of things, this is a pretty healthy lasagna dish and has some amazing flavors and textures.

Servings: 6 (9 x 13-inch baking dish) | Prep Time: 30 minutes | Total Time: 1 hour 15 minutes

1 medium yellow squash

1 medium zucchini

1 medium eggplant

Olive oil

Salt and pepper

1 pound lasagna noodles

16 ounces fresh ricotta cheese

8 ounces mozzarella cheese

1 lemon, zest and juice

4 cups marinara sauce

1 cup grated Parmesan cheese

1. Preheat oven to 350°F.

2. Slice the squash, zucchini, and eggplant horizontally so you have long strips of thin veggies. Shoot for slices that are about ¼ inch thick.

3. Lay out the eggplant on one baking sheet and the zucchini and squash on another. Drizzle with olive oil and salt. Bake the veggies for 10 minutes. The eggplant might need an extra 5 minutes.

4. Turn up the oven heat to 400°F.

5. Cook lasagna noodles according to package. They should be slightly undercooked. If you are pressed for time, feel free to use the no-cook noodles that are available in most stores.

6. Combine the ricotta cheese, mozzarella, and lemon zest and juice.

7. Add a few spoonfuls of sauce to the bottom of your lasagna pan and then lay in a layer of lasagna noodles. Don't worry if some are broken; just get a nice solid layer in the pan.

8. Next add your eggplant slices to the pan. If they won't all fit, make them fit! Try not to overlap them though. Then add one-third of your cheese mixture and drizzle a thin layer of sauce over it.

9. Next add another layer of noodles, the squash and zucchini slices, another third of the cheese mixture, and more sauce. Again, you can really squeeze the veggies in there, but try not to overlap.

10. For the top layer, add more noodles and the rest of the sauce and the cheese mixture. Spread Parmesan cheese on top and sprinkle with salt and pepper.

11. Bake the lasagna until edges are browned, about 30 to 35 minutes. Let the dish cool for 5 minutes before slicing and serving.

Note: Why bake the veggies before adding them to your lasagna? Because vegetables are mostly water, and it's important to cook out some of that water before adding them to the dish, or you'll end up with a big, wet, soggy mess.

Tomato Poached Cod

Fish is kind of hard to make in large amounts because most types of fish (most, but not all) just don't keep that well and are hard to reheat and reuse. But you can definitely use fish with other leftover dishes.

Tomato sauce and fish pair nicely together, and poaching the fish in the sauce keeps it super-moist and tender. Plus, it picks up some of that delicious saucy flavor.

Servings: 4 | Prep Time: 10 minutes | Total Time: 30 minutes

1. Preheat oven to 350°F.

2. Reheat marinara sauce on the stovetop until it's simmering. Thin the sauce with some white wine or water so it isn't quite as thick.

3. Slice off stems from the fennel bulb and then chop in half vertically. Save the greens for a garnish. Remove the more fibrous center of the fennel bulb, then turn the bulb on its side and slice thin. Halve the lemon and slice thin.

4. Pour marinara sauce in a large casserole dish (2-quart or 8 x 8-inch dish works well). You should have about a ¼-inch layer of sauce in the pan.

5. Nestle your fish fillets into the sauce and surround them with fennel and lemon slices. Sprinkle with a bit of salt and drizzle the whole dish with olive oil.

6. Bake the dish until the fish is cooked through, 20 to 25 minutes, depending on how thick your fillets are. When the fish starts to flake apart, it's done. The fennel should be a bit soft as well.

7. Serve the fish immediately with the sauce and fennel, with rice or couscous as a side. I like to use the small fennel greens as a garnish for the fish.

2 cups marinara sauce

½ cup white wine or water

1 fennel bulb

1 lemon

4 (6-ounce) fillets cod, or other white fish (tilapia works well also)

Sea salt or kosher salt

Olive oil

Fennel greens, garnish

Weeknight Bolognese

Italian grandmothers around the world might think this is sacrilege, but I'll say it anyway: You don't necessarily need to spend an entire day of your life to make a good Bolognese. Heck, you've already spent a day of your life making a great marinara sauce!

Is this sauce as succulent and wonderful as a pot of meat sauce that has been simmering all day? No. I won't claim that. But it's close, takes a fraction of the time, and is a perfect meal for a Tuesday!

Servings: 6 | Prep Time: 30 minutes | Total Time: 50 minutes

6 ounces bacon (about 5 thick strips), diced

1 pound ground beef

½ cup red wine

3 cups marinara sauce

1 pound pasta (spaghetti)

½ cup pasta water

Salt and pepper

Parmesan cheese, grated

1. Add diced bacon to a large pot over medium-low heat. Cook until most of the fat has rendered out and the bacon is getting browned, about 8 minutes.

2. Add ground beef to the pan and turn up heat to medium-high. Let meat brown well. Try not to stir it too much, letting it sear. But every few minutes you can give it a stir so it doesn't burn. Cook until it's well browned all around, probably 10 minutes.

3. Add red wine to the pan, using the liquid to scrape up any bits of beef or bacon stuck to the pan. Then add marinara sauce and bring to a simmer. Turn heat down to medium-low.

4. Cook pasta according to package while sauce simmers.

5. When pasta is done, scoop out ½ cup pasta water and add it to the sauce, then taste and adjust for salt and pepper. It might need a pinch of both.

6. Drain the pasta and pour it right into the Bolognese sauce. Mix it around well with tongs so the pasta is coated with the sauce. Serve immediately with grated Parmesan cheese.

Note: If you're using a jarred marinara sauce for this recipe, it's a good idea to dice a small onion and add it to the pan when the bacon is almost done crisping. It will add some extra depth and flavor to the sauce.

CHAPTER 7
LENTILS

After I graduated from college, I lived in a group house in Washington, DC. For those unfamiliar with group houses, it's normally four or five postgraduate people who wish they were still in college, so they establish small college-like living environments in major cities.

Those were some of the most fun years I've ever had, but it was pretty hard on the liver.

For a few years I lived in this group house with a friend who was absolutely obsessed with lentils. She would cook big pots of them and eat them for days, putting them in soups and stews—she even introduced me to the lentil cookie!

I remember one day getting upset with her for making such healthy food, so I grabbed all her lentils and made a big pot of MAN LENTILS (yes, you need to write it in all caps). They had sausage, bacon, and beer, and I believe some whiskey. They were actually pretty good, which just goes to show the versatility of the common lentil. Even when you try to sabotage them, they turn out okay.

There's no recipe for MAN LENTILS in this chapter because I just gave you the recipe: sausage, bacon, beer, whiskey, lentils. Consider it a bonus recipe.

After I started really getting into cooking, I realized that my friend was on to something. Lentils truly are one of the most versatile foods out there. You can use them to thicken and stuff or fill things, or you can just eat them with a spoon.

The one disclaimer I'll make about these tiny legumes—and I'm writing this only because my wife made me—is that they tend to make a mess. They are tiny and often bounce around. Spilling a bag of lentils, which you will inevitably do if you make enough of them, takes approximately two months to clean up. I still find spare lentils in random parts of my house from when I was working on recipes for this chapter. But that warning from my wife shouldn't deter you. Start cooking lentils regularly and you'll never stop.

Basic Lentils

It's a bit hard to give one recipe for lentils. There's a wide range of varieties, and all of them have slightly different textures and cooking times. The most popular ones in the United States (at least where I've lived) are the green and red lentils. You can also find French (*puy*) lentils and a few other varieties at some specialty stores.

It doesn't matter which variety you choose to use for the recipes in this chapter. They all work, but just vary a bit by taste and texture. Sometimes I even like to cook two different kinds and mix them up to make a multi-lentil dish.

Preparing Lentils

Regardless of which variety of lentil you purchase, make sure that you rinse them well before cooking them. Lentils can be dirty things. Also, it's a good idea to pick through them quickly to check for hard debris or rocks mixed in with the lentils. Sometimes that happens.

Once you've cleaned your lentils, just add them to a pot with the recommended amount of water. Usually that's about 2 to 3 cups of water for each cup of lentils. There's no need to soak lentils like other dried legumes. You can cook them right away.

Bring the lentils to a boil and then reduce the heat so the water is just barely simmering. If you have a heavy simmer or a boil, then your lentils will lose their form as they cook, and you'll wind up with a big pot of mush. Cooking time can vary wildly on lentils, from 10 minutes to 40 minutes.

Finishing Lentils

When your lentils are done cooking, they should be tender but not mushy at all. Drain them when you're happy with their texture and season with a bit of salt. If you're serving these lentils on their own as a side dish, I also recommend stirring in a small knob of butter and maybe a drizzle of olive oil. You can keep extra lentils for up to a week in the fridge.

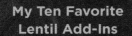

My Ten Favorite
Lentil Add-Ins

Bacon

Chives

Cilantro

Cream

Garlic

Leeks

Lemon

Sherry vinegar

Sorrel or spinach

Walnuts

Spicy Lentil Salad/Dip

This is one of those fantastic recipes that can work for any part of a meal. If you need an appetizer, serve it in a big bowl with tortilla chips. If you need a side dish, then just serve it with a large spoon. For a main dish, serve it over a large, soft pita bread. It's a great weeknight meal or weekday lunch. This recipe is reason enough to start cooking lentils regularly.

Servings: 4 as a main dish or 8 as a dip | Prep Time: 15 minutes | Total Time: 25 minutes

1 pound fingerling or new potatoes

½ red onion

1 cucumber, seeded

1 pint cherry tomatoes

8 radishes

1–2 jalapeños, seeded

4 cups cooked lentils

1 teaspoon paprika

¼ teaspoon cayenne pepper

⅓ cup olive oil

Salt and pepper

Garnishes

Avocado

Chips

Cilantro

Greek yogurt

Limes

Parsley

Pitas

1. Boil potatoes in salted water until tender, about 15 minutes.

2. Meanwhile, dice the onions and cucumber, quarter the cherry tomatoes, thinly slice the radishes, and mince the jalapeños.

3. When potatoes are done, chop and combine with veggies. Stir in lentils and paprika and cayenne. Drizzle with olive oil and season well with salt and pepper.

4. Serve with pita or chips and top with any of the garnishes.

Ten-Minute Lentil Wraps

Lentils can be almost meaty, even more so than beans, I think. There's something about them that is completely filling, which makes them great for a vegetarian lunch option.

Any time I have lentils on hand, I like to mix them with some veggies and stuff the whole shebang inside a few tortillas for a quick and healthy lunch.

Besides the basic wrap ingredients I've listed below, feel free to use almost any crunchy vegetable. As long as you shred it or slice it very thin, it'll work well in these wraps.

Servings: 4 wraps | Prep Time: 10 minutes | Total Time: 10 minutes

1. Mix lentils with feta cheese. Add a drizzle of olive oil and season well with salt and pepper.

2. Lay a tortilla flat and add some spinach to the middle. Top with red onions, sprouts, and the lentil mixture.

3. Fold the ends of the tortilla over and roll the wrap away from you. Try to keep it nice and tight so the ingredients don't fall out.

4. You can either serve these whole or slice them up for a tasty appetizer.

2 cups cooked lentils

½ cup crumbled feta cheese

Olive oil

Salt and pepper

Large flour tortillas

Baby spinach

½ cup slivered red onions

Sprouts

Curried Lentils and Carrots

Carrots rarely get to be the star of the show, but their flavor is fantastic in this dish. The lentils give the dish some body, but the curry powder–carrot combination makes it delicious.

The most crucial elements of this recipe are the brown sugar and the lemon juice. The sugar caramelizes slightly and brings out the sweetness in the carrots, and the acid from the lemon juice helps all the flavors pop. This would be a great side dish to serve with almost any cut of meat, but would work best with a nice steak or lamb cut.

Servings: 4 as a side | Prep Time: 5 minutes | Total Time: 20 minutes

1 cup peeled and sliced carrots

2 tablespoons unsalted butter

2 cups cooked lentils

1 tablespoon curry powder

2 teaspoons brown sugar

Salt and pepper

1 tablespoon lemon juice

1. When you slice the carrots, aim for ¼-inch thickness. Steam carrots until they are barely soft, about 5 minutes.

2. Melt butter in a medium pan over medium heat. Add steamed carrots to pan and cook for a minute or two in the melted butter. Stir in lentils along with curry powder. Cook for a few more minutes. Add brown sugar and a pinch of salt and pepper.

3. To finish, squeeze on the fresh lemon juice. Serve immediately.

Stuffed Portobello Mushrooms

I originally thought of these as a hearty side dish, but after making them a few times, I think they are more of a meal. An entire stuffed mushroom plus a side salad is a pretty filling plate, and I don't think you'll be disappointed with the flavors.

If you are crunched for time, make the filling and stuff these mushrooms in advance and then just toss them in the oven when you're ready for dinner. The prepared 'shrooms will keep fine in the fridge for a day or two.

Servings: 4 | Prep Time: 20 minutes | Total Time: 50 minutes

1. Preheat oven to 400°F.

2. In a large skillet, add a drizzle of olive oil over medium heat. Add the garlic and fresh spinach. Pour a few tablespoons of water into the pan to help the spinach cook down.

3. Once spinach is cooked down, stir in lentils and season with salt, pepper, lemon juice, and a dash of hot sauce (if you're using it). Stir until lentils are warmed, just a minute or two.

4. Remove mixture from heat and stir in feta cheese.

5. Lay out four cleaned large portobello mushrooms in a baking dish and drizzle them lightly with olive oil. Divide lentil filling between mushrooms and top each mushroom with bread crumbs. The filling should overfill the mushrooms.

6. Bake stuffed mushrooms until mushrooms are softened and bread crumbs are lightly toasted, about 30 minutes. Serve immediately with a side salad.

2 tablespoons olive oil, divided

2 cloves garlic, minced

1 bunch (about 4 packed cups) fresh spinach

1½ cups cooked lentils

Salt and pepper

½ lemon, juice only

Hot sauce (optional)

4 ounces crumbled feta cheese

4 large portobello mushrooms

½ cup panko bread crumbs

Indian Dal

Normally with Indian dishes, you cook (or order) a number of different dishes and then everyone shares, family style. Good dal, which is normally just spiced lentils, is one of my favorite dishes. In fact, I like it so much that my wife and I normally can make a meal out of just this dish and a good amount of na'an flatbread.

This is a really quick recipe and produces a finished product that can rival all but the best Indian restaurants.

Servings: 2 as a main dish or 4 as a side | Prep Time: 10 minutes | Total Time: 20 minutes

2 tablespoons butter or ghee

3 cups cooked lentils

1 inch fresh ginger, grated

1½ cups tomato puree or sauce

1 cup water

1 teaspoon ground coriander

¼ teaspoon cayenne pepper

2 tablespoons minced cilantro

½ cup heavy cream

Salt and pepper

Na'an bread

Melted butter or ghee for brushing na'an

1. Add butter or ghee (clarified butter) to a medium saucepan over medium heat. Once it's melted, add the lentils and ginger, letting them cook until warmed through, roughly 2 to 3 minutes.

2. Add tomato puree and water and bring to a simmer. Add coriander, cayenne, and cilantro and let simmer for a few minutes until the sauce starts to thicken.

3. Add cream and simmer; dal should continue to thicken. Season with salt and pepper and serve with na'an.

Note: While you can make na'an from scratch, I'm usually able to find a very good version in the bakery section of my grocery store. It's already cooked through, so you just bake it (or grill it) for a few minutes and then brush with some melted butter. It's delicious, and I can eat my weight in it. Perfect for sopping up all the delicious dal sauce. In a pinch, warmed pitas work well also.

Thirty-Minute Lentil Stew

Honestly, this stew doesn't take very long even if you start with dried lentils. Using cooked lentils almost makes it too easy. You could make this sucker on a Tuesday after working a double. It's just that easy. Thirty minutes estimates that you are the slowest person on earth. I bet you can bust this out in even less time and have a delicious and healthy dinner on the table.

In my opinion, the cumin yogurt isn't really optional for this dish. The stew really needs this lemony, creamy addition to round out all the flavors. In other words, the yogurt takes this stew to another level.

Servings: 4 | Prep Time: 10 minutes | Total Time: 30 minutes

1. **For cumin yogurt:** Mix ingredients together in a small bowl and store in the fridge until needed.

2. **To make the stew:** Add olive oil to a large pot over medium heat. Once oil is hot, add onions and carrots and a pinch of salt. Cook vegetables until they begin to soften, about 5 minutes.

3. Add lentils, tomatoes with liquid, and broth to the pot and bring to a simmer. Let simmer for 5 minutes to allow the flavors to combine.

4. Rinse the kale or Swiss chard and cut out the thick rib in the leaves. Very roughly chop the leaves. Add kale or chard to the pot and cook for another minute or two so the greens are wilted.

5. Season with salt and pepper and serve with cumin yogurt on top.

Cumin Spiced Yogurt

1 cup Greek yogurt

1 teaspoon ground cumin

1 tablespoon lemon juice

Pinch of salt

2 tablespoons olive oil

1 medium yellow onion, diced

2 medium carrots, peeled and diced

Salt and pepper

3 cups cooked lentils

1 (28-ounce) can diced tomatoes

2 cups vegetable broth

1 bunch kale or Swiss chard

Seared Salmon with Caper Lentils

Lentils present another great opportunity to sneak some seafood into a leftover plan. Lentils pair really well with heartier seafood, like salmon. The salmon in this recipe is lightly pan-seared, and the lentils are mixed with capers and lemon to incorporate some classic flavors that work really well with fish. The end result is a restaurant-quality meal that's ready in less than thirty minutes.

Note: It's a great idea to pair this recipe with the Herb-Roasted Salmon recipe in chapter 13 if you have leftovers.

Servings: 4 | Prep Time: 15 minutes | Total Time: 30 minutes

Salmon

4 (4-ounce) fillets of salmon, skin on

2 tablespoons olive oil

Kosher salt

2 tablespoons unsalted butter

Lemon wedges, for serving

Lentils

2 tablespoons olive oil

½ cup white or yellow diced onions

½ cup diced celery

½ cup diced carrots

2 cloves garlic, minced

Salt and pepper

2 cups cooked lentils

¼ cup capers (optional)

1 teaspoon fresh thyme

2 tablespoons unsalted butter

Juice of ½ lemon

1. Preheat oven to 350°F.

2. Lightly drizzle salmon with olive oil and sprinkle with salt.

3. Add salmon fillets, skin side up, to a hot, oven-safe pan over high heat on the stove. Sear fillets for about 3 minutes per side.

4. After searing fillets, turn them skin side down and add a small knob of butter to each fillet. Stick pan in the oven and finish cooking for about 5 to 7 minutes. The total time will depend on the thickness of your salmon.

5. **To prepare the lentils:** Add olive oil to a large pan over medium-high heat. Once hot, add the onions, celery, and carrots. Cook until veggies are softened, about 5 minutes. Add garlic and a pinch of salt and continue to cook for another minute.

6. Stir in cooked lentils, capers (if you're using them), and fresh thyme. Cook for another few minutes to warm everything.

7. Add butter and lemon juice to the pan and season with salt and pepper.

8. Serve salmon on a bed of the lentil mixture. Garnish with lemon wedges.

Mini Samosas

If you're ever stuck for ways to jazz up leftovers, it's probably a good bet that wrapping them in eggroll wrappers and frying them will make for good eats.

While lentils are a standard filling for samosas, potatoes are equally delicious. If you happen to have some leftover potatoes handy, toss them in with the mix!

Servings: 40–45 small samosas, or 12 large eggrolls or samosas | Prep Time: 30 minutes | Total Time: 50 minutes

1–2 Serrano or bird chiles, seeded and minced

3 scallions, minced

¼ cup minced fresh mint

¼ cup minced fresh cilantro

3 cups cooked lentils

Pinch of salt

15 eggroll wrappers

1 quart oil for frying

Chili Ketchup

1 cup ketchup

2 tablespoons chili garlic sauce

1. Remove seeds from chiles and dice them finely. Add scallions, mint, and cilantro to the peppers. Add lentils to the mix and season with a pinch of salt.

2. Working with one eggroll wrapper at a time, slice it into thirds so you have long strips of wrapper.

3. Take one of the strips and fold the bottom corner up to form a triangle. Fold that triangle up to form a small pouch with the wrapper. Carefully pick up the wrapper so the pouch stays formed and stuff in about 2 tablespoons of lentil filling.

4. After the wrapper is filled, continue rolling the triangle up. For the last fold, rub some cold water on the wrapper so the last fold sticks well and seals the samosa.

5. Repeat with all the wrappers. You should be able to get at least forty small samosas.

6. Add oil to a large, heavy pot and heat to 350°F. Use a deep-fry thermometer to make sure your oil is the right temperature.

7. Fry samosas until they are a deep golden brown, about 5 minutes. Work in batches depending on the size of your pot, and make sure your oil heats up again between batches.

8. When the samosas come out of the fryer, let them drain on a paper towel for a minute or two.

9. Serve samosas immediately with spicy mustard, soy sauce, and/or chili ketchup.

Lentil Cookies

Desserts are hard to pull off for leftover dishes, unless of course you're reading the dessert chapter (ice cream)! Other than that, you won't see too many sweet recipes in this book.

These cookies are a huge exception to that rule. They are some of the healthiest cookies I've ever made and, in spite of their healthiness, are packed with flavor and have a wonderful texture. And don't worry, you can't really taste the lentils. They just give the cookies some real body, making them especially filling. Definitely save a cup of lentils for these bad boys.

Servings: 30 cookies | Prep Time: 20 minutes | Total Time: 40 minutes

1. Preheat oven to 375°F.

2. Bring lentils and water to a simmer in a small pan. As the lentils simmer, mash them with a fork to form a lentil paste. Set this aside and let it cool.

3. In a medium bowl, combine the flours, cinnamon, nutmeg, baking powder, and salt. Mix well to combine.

4. In the bowl for a stand mixer (or a normal mixing bowl if you're using a hand mixer), cream together the butter and sugars until mixture is light and fluffy. Slowly mix in the egg, almond extract, and cooled lentil mash.

5. Slowly stir in the dry ingredients and mix until combined. Try not to overmix the batter. Finally, stir in the oats, dried fruit, and coconut.

6. Scoop heaping tablespoon-size balls of batter onto baking sheets lined with parchment paper. Leave about an inch in between the cookies.

7. Bake cookies until lightly browned, 16 to 18 minutes.

8. Let cool briefly before eating! If you want to store the leftovers, let them cool completely and store in a plastic bag or Tupperware container.

1 cup cooked lentils

1 cup water

1 cup all-purpose flour

1 cup whole wheat flour

1 teaspoon cinnamon

½ teaspoon ground nutmeg

1 teaspoon baking powder

½ teaspoon table salt

1 cup (2 sticks) unsalted butter

½ cup sugar

½ cup light brown sugar

1 large egg

2 teaspoons almond extract

1 cup rolled oats

1 cup dried fruit (cranberries or raisins or both)

1 cup unsweetened shredded coconut

CHAPTER 8

BREAD

Do me a favor: The next time you buy sliced sandwich bread at the store, take a second to turn over the bag and check out the ingredient list. My guess is that it will have more than ten and probably closer to fifteen ingredients.

This baffles me because good, homemade bread really needs just four: flour, yeast, water, and salt. Anything else is above and beyond. In the case of the fifteen ingredients that are normally in your store-bought sliced bread, they are most likely preservatives and dough softeners.

In my opinion, good bread should be neither softened nor preserved. Instead of soft, it should be crusty, sturdy, and firm. It should stand up to the thickest sandwich or spread without falling apart. And a loaf of bread shouldn't last a month. At most it should last two weeks, and that's only if you don't mind stale bread for the last week or so.

Of course, most people think there's no way around it. To make bread at home takes too much time and too much equipment. Who wants to slave away for hours sifting and kneading and rising?

Who has time for that?

I'll be the first to admit that I definitely don't.

But I still make at least one, and normally two, loaves of homemade bread every single month. The bread I make requires no kneading and very little work, and is way cheaper than store-bought stuff.

And it's also amazingly flavorful and useful.

In my mind, bread is a fundamental leftover dish. It's probably one of the oldest prepared foods and can be used for hundreds of things. This chapter is just a start, but it should be enough to convince you to try a loaf of homemade bread and see where it can take you.

No-Knead Bread

Some people will question the benefits of making bread at home. It's just so much easier to pick up a sliced loaf from the supermarket. But there really is nothing like a nice loaf of crusty, rustic bread, and this recipe makes baking homemade bread about as easy as it can be.

I can make a killer lunch out of a few good slices of this bread with some cheese, hummus, or other spreads. Slice it into wedges, and it's a show-stopping appetizer.

Deliciousness aside, this loaf also costs less than $1 to make. Good luck finding a rustic loaf of bread for that price at your local bakery or grocery store.

Servings: Makes 1 large loaf | Prep Time: 10 minutes | Total Time: 1 hour plus overnight rise and second-day 1-hour rise

4 cups bread flour (you can also sub up to 2 of those cups with whole wheat flour)

⅓ teaspoon active dry yeast

1½ teaspoons kosher salt

2¼ cups cool water

Extra flour for dusting

Fine cornmeal (optional)

1. In a large bowl, mix together flour, yeast, and salt.

2. Stir in water and mix with your hand until it forms a very loose dough. It should be too wet to knead. It is supposed to be sticky, but it's okay if it still holds its shape a bit. If the dough seems dry, add a few more tablespoons of water. Don't stress too much about the consistency. It's a flexible loaf.

3. Cover the bowl loosely with plastic wrap or a towel and let it rise at room temperature for 14 to 18 hours. In a pinch, I've continued with as little as 10 hours of rise time.

4. After the overnight rise, dust the dough and countertop liberally with flour and turn the dough out onto the counter. Fold the dough over itself a few times to shape it into a ball.

5. Place the dough ball on a kitchen towel dusted with fine cornmeal or flour. There should be a seam in the dough where you folded the edges together. Put this seam down on the towel, so the top of the dough ball is smooth. Fold the edges of the towel up to cover the dough and let it rise for at least an hour, but up to 2 hours.

6. About 30 minutes before you are ready to bake your loaf, place a large, cast-iron dutch oven into the oven without the lid and preheat oven to 500°F.

7. After preheating, remove the dutch oven and turn dough into the hot pot. The seam of the bread should be facing up. Cover with the lid. Bake, covered, for 30 minutes.

8. Carefully remove lid and bake until the crust is a deep brown, another 15 minutes. I like a really deep-browned crust, so I usually will leave mine in for an extra 5 minutes.

9. Carefully remove loaf from pan and cool on a wire rack for at least 30 minutes before slicing.

Storing the Bread

Once your loaf is cool, you can store it at room temperature wrapped loosely for a day or two. After that it will start to go stale. I prefer to keep mine in a plastic bag in the fridge. It will keep for 2 weeks, although it will start to get stale after a week. Some recipes actually work better if you use stale bread. Bread also freezes nicely, so feel free to freeze half a loaf and defrost it slowly when needed. It might lose some of its crunchy exterior, but will still be tasty.

Note on dutch oven lids: Most lids that come with dutch ovens have warnings about being exposed to extreme temperatures. The cast iron lid itself can take the 500°F temperature for this recipe, but the plastic knob on the lid will possibly melt. To solve this problem, you can purchase a steel replacement knob on-line or in most specialty stores for a few bucks and then your pot will be ready for the high temperatures.

Four No-Knead Bread Variations

These variations are all prepared the same way as the main No-Knead Bread recipe. Just add the flavoring ingredients to the normal bread recipe.

VARIATION	INGREDIENTS	PREPARATION
Roasted Garlic Bread	2 whole heads of garlic 1 tablespoon olive oil Kosher salt	Cut off stem ends of garlic bulbs. Wrap them loosely in foil and drizzle on some olive oil and a pinch of kosher salt. Close up the foil and bake at 350°F for 30 minutes. When cool, remove the roasted cloves from the skins and mash them together with the dry ingredients for the bread. Continue with the bread recipe as normal.
Cheese Bread	8 ounces semi-hard cheese 1 teaspoon black pepper	Use a nice semi-hard cheese for this recipe. Something like pecorino works well. Cut off any rind pieces and then cube the cheese into ¼-inch cubes. Mix cheese cubes and pepper with dry ingredients for bread and continue with recipe as normal.
Olive Bread	1½–2 cups kalamata olives, roughly chopped Omit salt from original recipe	The olives are very salty so you can leave out the salt from the original recipe. Add olives to dry recipe ingredients and continue with recipe as normal.
Bacon Bread	2 cups crumbled crispy bacon, about 8 thick strips ½ teaspoon red pepper flakes	Add bacon and red pepper flakes to the original dry ingredients and mix well. Continue with the normal recipe.

Toad in a Hole

Like most leftover recipes, the ones in this chapter can work with almost any leftover bread that you happen to have around. That said, I did try to pick recipes that work best with a nice, crusty bread like the one you'll get out of your no-knead loaf.

For my money, there's no better way to start the day than with a few slices of buttered crusty bread alongside a few perfectly cooked, over-easy eggs. This dish is a spin on that meal, but the eggs actually cook in your bread slice.

It's fun to break off a toast end and dip it in the center of the egg. Kids will love this recipe!

Servings: 2 | Prep Time: 5 minutes | Total Time: 10 minutes

1. Slice four ½-inch pieces of no-knead bread. Any bread variation would work great for this dish.

2. Lightly butter both sides of each slice and use a cookie cutter to cut a hole in the center of each piece, or simply use a knife to cut a circle in it.

3. In a large, nonstick skillet or griddle, add in as many pieces of bread as will fit. Cook the bread over medium-high heat for about 3 minutes.

4. Flip the pieces of bread and crack an egg into the hole of each slice. Cook for another 2 to 3 minutes. The egg should be mostly set at this point.

5. If you have a lid for your pan, cover the pan and let the eggs steam for about a minute to set the whites. Alternatively, you can carefully flip the bread again and cook for about 15 seconds on the last side for an over-easy egg. Cook longer if you like your yolk hard.

6. Serve with a sprinkle of salt and pepper.

4 slices bread
Butter
4 large eggs
Salt and pepper

Garlic Croutons

One way to save stale bread from the garbage can is to make it even more stale!

In just a few minutes, you can toss some super-stale bread (or fresh if you can't wait) with a few simple ingredients and make a delicious topping for any salad. The good news is that once these croutons are baked, they will extend the life of your bread for weeks!

Servings: Makes 2 cups | Prep Time: 5 minutes | Total Time: 20 minutes

2 heaping cups ¼-inch cubed bread (about 2 thick slices)

1–2 cloves garlic

1 teaspoon kosher salt

2 tablespoons olive oil

Black pepper

1. Preheat oven to 400°F.

2. Mince the garlic and then add it to a bowl with the salt. Use a fork to mash the garlic and salt together to form a rough paste. Add in olive oil and a pinch of ground pepper. Stir together well.

3. Toss bread cubes with the olive oil and garlic mixture.

4. Scoop croutons onto a baking sheet and bake for 15 minutes. Give them a stir after every 5 minutes or so to make sure they are cooking evenly.

5. Remove the croutons and let them cool before serving. They will get nice and crunchy as they cool.

6. You can store the croutons in a plastic bag for a week or two.

A Sweet Version

Sometimes I like to create a sweet crouton, which makes for a great cereal topping. Instead of the ingredients listed above, toss the bread with ¼ cup melted butter and sprinkle with 2 tablespoons sugar and 2 teaspoons cinnamon. Bake at a lower 300°F until bread is lightly browned and crispy, 20 to 25 minutes. Stir the croutons a few times as they bake to make sure they are cooking evenly.

The croutons will have a great cinnamon-sugar flavor that will work well with milk on granola or any cereal.

Sun-Dried Tomato Panzanella Salad

Panzanella salad is a classic way to use stale bread. In fact, you have to have stale bread to make it. Fresh bread just won't work. This salad is traditionally made with very fresh and ripe summer tomatoes, and you can definitely use those if they are in season. But by substituting sun-dried tomatoes for the summer tomatoes, you can make this recipe any time of the year.

I like to keep my version of this salad simple, but the salad is flexible and you should feel free to add any veggies that fit your fancy. Try artichoke hearts, chickpeas, or fresh sweet corn.

Servings: 4 as an appetizer | Prep Time: 15 minutes | Total Time: 25 minutes

1. Add stale bread pieces to a bowl and toss with olive oil and oil from sun-dried tomatoes. Stir well to coat bread.

2. Add sun-dried tomatoes to the bowl along with cucumber and onions. Add fresh basil and lemon juice, and season well with salt and pepper.

3. Let the salad sit at room temperature for 10 to 15 minutes before serving.

Note: If you just can't wait for your bread to get stale, you can rip up fresh bread and bake it in a 300°F oven for 15 minutes. Your goal is to dry the bread out, but not make it crunchy like croutons.

3 cups stale bread (about 3 large slices), ripped into pieces

2 tablespoons good olive oil

3 tablespoons oil from the sun-dried tomatoes

⅓ cup finely diced sun-dried tomatoes from oil

1 medium cucumber, peeled and seeded

¼ cup diced red onion

¼ cup minced fresh basil

½ lemon, juice only

Salt and pepper

The A.B.L.E. Sandwich

The BLT is a classic sandwich, one for which I don't need to give you instructions.

This version, however, omits the tomato. While this may seem sacrilege, what's nice about it is that you can make the A.B.L.E. (Avocado, Bacon, Lettuce, Egg) Sandwich even when tomatoes aren't in season. If you do have good tomatoes, feel free to add them and make a T.A.B.L.E. Sandwich.

Biting into this sandwich and having the over-easy egg run together with the bacon and creamy avocado creates one of my favorite sandwich flavor combos.

Servings: 1 large sandwich | Prep Time: 20 minutes | Total Time: 20 minutes

3-4 strips thick bacon

2 large slices sturdy bread (or 4 standard slices)

Bacon grease

1-2 eggs

½ ripe avocado

Green leaf lettuce

Note: Don't toast the bread in a toaster if you brush it with grease. It will burn.

1. Cook bacon in a skillet, on a griddle, or in a 350°F oven until very crispy (about 20 minutes if you use the oven). Remove bacon and reserve the bacon grease.

2. Brush your bread with a small amount of bacon grease and toast in the oven or in a skillet until lightly browned on each side.

3. Add a teaspoon of bacon grease or butter to a small, nonstick skillet over medium-high heat. Once hot, crack in two eggs and cook for about 90 seconds. Then flip each egg and cook for another 15 to 20 seconds. This will make a nice over-easy egg, which I recommend for a sandwich since the yolk makes a sauce.

4. To assemble the sandwich, scoop avocado onto one piece of bread and spread it out well. Add lettuce next, then bacon, and finally the two eggs (one for each half of the sandwich). You may only want to fry one egg, but I like to go big.

5. Top the sandwich with the other piece of bread, slice it in half, and chow down.

Using Bacon Grease

Like duck fat, rendered bacon fat is a fantastic cooking tool. Brushing a bit on bread before toasting it gives the whole sandwich a subtle but deep bacon flavor. When using bacon grease, be sure to control your heat, as the fat can burn. Don't ever put it in the toaster unless you like using fire extinguishers.

Spanish Migas

Migas are one of those foods that vary widely depending on where you eat them. There are some Tex-Mex versions made with eggs and corn tortillas, but this recipe has Spanish roots. What you'll notice about a lot of the leftover bread recipes, including this one, is that they can work for a variety of meals. This dish is originally a tapas-style meal, but I really like it for breakfast. If you're making it for breakfast, try it with a few fried eggs.

Servings: 4 | Prep Time: 15 minutes | Total Time: 35 minutes

4 cups torn bread (4–6 slices)

⅔ cup cold water

1 pound spicy chorizo

½ red pepper, minced

2 cloves garlic, minced

3–4 tablespoons olive oil

Salt and pepper

Smoked paprika

4 large eggs (optional)

Note: If you want the migas to be more rustic, leave the crusty ends on, but you can also remove them. I leave them on because I like the texture, and it's more work to remove them.

1. Toss the bread pieces with the cold water and let them sit for 10 minutes or so. Some pieces might get soggier than others and that's okay.

2. In a large skillet over medium-high heat, add chorizo (removed from casing) and cook until browned thoroughly, about 10 minutes. As it cooks, break up the chorizo with a spatula.

3. Once browned, remove chorizo from pan, leaving the grease. Add red pepper and garlic. Turn heat down to medium and cook until vegetables are soft, about 3 to 4 minutes.

4. If the pan is dry, add a good drizzle of olive oil. Depending on how much fat was in your sausage, you might need an extra tablespoon or two of oil.

5. Remove the cooked peppers and garlic so they don't burn and add the bread pieces to the skillet. Let the bread sit in the hot pan for 3 to 4 minutes so they start to brown nicely.

6. After the bread has browned a bit, return chorizo, peppers, and garlic to pan and continue to cook for another minute.

7. Season with salt and pepper and add a pinch of smoked paprika.

8. Optionally, remove the migas from the pan and crack in a few eggs. Fry them gently for 2 to 3 minutes and then flip them and cook for another 15 to 20 seconds so the yolks are still runny.

9. Serve migas with eggs.

Note: When the migas are done, the bread will have different textures. Some parts will be crispy and browned and some might be slightly soggy from the water and the oil from the pan. This is good. The bread will be very flavorful, and the different textures are really nice.

Corn/Bread Pudding

There's cornbread, there's bread pudding, and there's cornbread pudding (bread pudding made with cornbread). This is none of those things and all of those things at once. Just trust me that whatever it is, it's yummy.

One of the best ways to use up extra bread is to make a bread pudding. While a sweet version is the standard, I like to make a savory version that works either as a brunch or a dinner dish. While this version has corn and some spicy flavors, you can use almost any vegetable or cheese in this dish. Get creative!

Servings: 4 (8 x 8-inch baking dish) | Prep Time: 30 minutes | Total Time: 1 hour 30 minutes

1. Preheat oven to 350°F.

2. Butter an 8 x 8-inch baking dish. Layer pieces of stale bread in the buttered dish. If you don't have any really stale bread, toast your bread for 10 minutes as the oven preheats to dry it out.

3. Add grated cheddar (you could use any cheese, really) to the top of the bread chunks until it just barely covers them.

4. In a large skillet, heat oil over medium-high heat. Once hot, add onions, red pepper, corn, and Serrano pepper. Cook for a few minutes until veggies soften. Season with a pinch of salt.

5. In a separate bowl, whisk together eggs, milk, and cornmeal.

6. Add cooked veggies to casserole dish. Then pour custard egg mixture over the bread and veggies. Top dish with fresh thyme, salt, and pepper.

7. Cover the dish with foil and let it rest for at least 15 minutes, or you can prepare the casserole to this point the night before you intend to bake it.

8. Bake, covered, for 20 minutes and then uncovered for 30 minutes. The dish is done when the custard in the center is set.

9. Let cool for a minute or two and then serve!

Butter for dish

4 cups (4-6 slices) torn stale bread

1½ cups grated cheddar cheese

1 tablespoon olive or vegetable oil

½ yellow onion, diced

½ red pepper, diced

2 cups (about 3 ears) sweet corn

1 Serrano pepper, minced (seeds optional)

Salt and pepper

4 large eggs

2 cups milk

¼ cup cornmeal

1 teaspoon fresh thyme

Note: If you want a spicier dish, leave the pepper seeds in. Otherwise, scrape them out.

Chorizo Bread Soup

Before I tried it, I was very skeptical about adding bread to a soup. Mind you, I don't mean serving the bread alongside the soup. I mean bread is actually an ingredient in this soup.

While that might sound weird, trust me on it. The bread mostly dissolves in the liquid and thickens the soup, giving it some richness. The end result is a hearty soup that's perfect for a cool winter night.

Servings: 4 | Prep Time: 20 minutes | Total Time: 40 minutes

8 ounces chorizo

2 tablespoons olive oil

½ yellow onion, diced

1 carrot, peeled and diced

1 stalk celery, diced

Salt and pepper

3 cloves garlic, minced

1 (28-ounce) can diced tomatoes

1 quart chicken or veggie stock

2 cups crusty bread, in ½-inch pieces

Fresh parsley, garnish (optional)

1. Remove chorizo from casing and cook sausage in a large pot over medium-high heat with olive oil. Cook until sausage is nicely browned, about 10 minutes.

2. Remove chorizo and add diced onions, carrots, and celery. Cook until veggies are soft, about 4 to 5 minutes. Add a pinch of salt. Add in minced garlic and cook for another minute.

3. Stir in tomatoes and stock and bring to a simmer. Stir chorizo back in and simmer for 5 minutes.

4. Add torn pieces of bread to soup. Simmer for 10 minutes, stirring occasionally. The bread will mostly dissolve, but some pieces will remain, which is fine.

5. Season with salt and pepper and garnish with a little chopped parsley if desired. Serve soup with extra bread or crackers.

The Lamb Loaf

This is not your mother's meatloaf. If you are a mother and make meatloaf, this is most likely not your meatloaf.

I grew up eating a lot of meatloaf, and what I usually think of when I think of meatloaf is blocks of meat drenched in grease and ketchup. Somehow most meatloaf manages to be dry and yet greasy. It's a kitchen marvel, really. Even if you don't use the lamb that this recipe calls for, just start cooking your meatloaf like this and you'll never go back. This method lets most of the grease drain away and uses a nice glaze to lock in moisture and flavor.

Servings: 6 | Prep Time: 30 minutes | Total Time: 1 hour 30 minutes

2 cups (3–4 slices) bread

1 tablespoon olive oil

1 yellow onion, diced

1 carrot, peeled and diced

3 cloves garlic, minced

2 pounds ground lamb

1 large egg

¼ cup minced fresh mint

¼ cup minced fresh parsley

1 teaspoon red pepper flakes

1 teaspoon paprika

Salt and pepper

Glaze

1 cup ketchup

1 teaspoon fresh thyme

2 teaspoons cumin seeds

2 tablespoons honey

1 dash hot sauce

1 dash Worcestershire sauce

1. Preheat oven to 350°F.

2. Rip bread into about ½-inch pieces and dry out in the preheating oven for 10 minutes. Then use either a food processor or your hands to crumble the bread.

3. In a large skillet, add olive oil over medium-high heat. Add onions, carrots, and garlic and cook until they are soft, about 5 minutes. Let veggies cool a bit before proceeding.

4. In a large bowl, combine cooked veggies with bread crumbs, lamb, the egg, and the herbs and spices. Season with a good pinch of salt and pepper and mix together well with your hands.

5. Press mixture into a 9-inch loaf pan. Flip loaf pan over onto a baking sheet lined with parchment paper and remove pan, leaving an inverted, freeform loaf on the sheet.

6. Bake the loaf for 45 minutes.

7. Whisk together the ingredients for the glaze while the loaf is baking.

8. After 45 minutes of baking, remove loaf from oven and pour off any pools of fat that have run off the meatloaf. Be careful when removing the fat if you choose to do this. I like to gently tilt the pan and use a spoon to scoop out any pools of fat.

9. Next, add a coat of glaze to the entire loaf. Reserve extra glaze for serving.

10. Return loaf to oven and turn heat up to 400°F. Bake for another 20 minutes.

11. Let loaf cool for 5 minutes and cut into thick slices. Slice the loaf in the middle first to make sure it's cooked through. Serve with extra glaze on the side.

Note: Ground lamb can be a bit pricey. Feel free to substitute ground beef for half or all of the lamb. If you substitute for all the lamb, remove the mint from the recipe. Heck, even half ground beef and half pork is a delicious alternative.

Leftovers Squared

If you have leftover meatloaf on day two, slice two pieces of no-knead bread and slather one piece with a bit of the extra glaze. Pile on a slice of leftover meatloaf. If you want to get crazy, add some grated cheese to the other piece of bread. Bake this in a 450°F oven until the meatloaf is hot. Best meatloaf sandwich ever!

CHAPTER 9
PULLED PORK

One weekend in early fall, I was cooking for a few friends and their parents who happened to be in town. The goal was to relax, watch some football, and eat great food. Instead we spent the day watching over a grilled eight-pound pork shoulder.

The six of us sat down to eat later and stuffed our faces with delicious pulled pork, flatbreads, coleslaw, and maybe more than one beer. The important part is that I thought we *killed* the pork shoulder. *How could there be any left?*

Then I went into the kitchen to find that we had barely dented the sucker. We were all completely stuffed, and the pork was almost laughing at us as if to say, "Is that all you got?!" It was, in fact, all we had.

Buying a pork shoulder (or butt—the same cut of meat) in the store can be intimidating, but cooking it couldn't be easier. Whether you do it on the grill, in the oven, or in the slow cooker, it's hard to screw up, and you'll have plenty of food for many wonderful meals. In fact, you'll probably want to freeze some, as eating a whole pork shoulder in one week is a tall order for a single family.

When buying a pork shoulder, look for one around eight to ten pounds. You can find them trimmed down to five or six pounds, but normally they trim off a lot of fat to make that weight and fat isn't a bad thing, especially if you're grilling or roasting it. Also, try to get the butt with the bone in (sometimes labeled as a picnic butt). Regardless of the method you use, the bone gives the meat much more flavor as it cooks. Keep it in if you can.

Sure, cooking a full pork shoulder takes some time. Actually, it takes about a day to do correctly, but it's worth it. It's very hard to screw up, and the leftovers are some of the best you'll find.

Grilled Pork Butt

I called this "grilled" because that's how I prefer to do it if I have the ability, but I've roasted the exact same recipe in the oven with excellent results. Either way you choose, be sure to get a pork butt (aka shoulder) with the bone in and with a decent amount of fat in it. As it cooks, the fat will prevent the meat from drying out and the bone will flavor the meat nicely.

Either this method or the slow cooker method yields delicious pulled pork. My personal preference is for grilling it—just because I like drier pulled pork that I can then add sauce to—but honestly, I'll take it any way I can get it!

Servings: makes about 6 pounds pulled pork, enough for about 30 sandwiches or 10–12 cups shredded pork | Prep Time: 20 minutes | Total Time: 10 hours plus optional overnight rest

1 tablespoon kosher salt

1 tablespoon brown sugar

1 tablespoon paprika

1 tablespoon red pepper flakes

1 tablespoon ground cumin

1 tablespoon coarsely ground black pepper

8-pound bone-in pork butt

Note: This recipe is almost impossible without a meat thermometer. You really can't judge the pork by sight or feel. A thermometer is the only way to know. Personally, I prefer a digital probe thermometer that can be left in the pork as it roasts or grills. When you insert the thermometer, stick it into the thickest part of the pork butt, and be sure not to have it next to any bone or you'll get a false reading.

1. Stir together the first six ingredients in a small bowl. Optionally, you can also try this recipe with any of the dry rub recipes from the Flank Steak chapter!

2. Rub the pork butt well with the spice mixture. It should completely cover the butt on all sides.

3. Tightly wrap the pork in plastic wrap and store in your fridge overnight. (This step isn't completely essential but does help the flavors mingle.)

4. Heat your grill or oven to 250°F. I highly recommend using an oven thermometer on the grill surface to make sure your temperature is as close to that as possible. If you're using a gas grill, this will probably mean turning off all the burners except one and turning that burner on medium-low to low. If you're using a charcoal grill, prepare your grill for indirect heat and build a good coal base before adding the pork. You will most likely have to add charcoal a few times throughout the cooking time to maintain a nice even heat. It's also not a huge deal if your grill gets hotter or cools off a bit. Just do your best to keep it low and steady.

5. Place your pork fat side up directly on the grill or in a roasting rack if you're roasting in the oven.

6. Cook the pork at 250°F until it reaches an internal temperature of 190° to 195°F. You absolutely need a meat thermometer to make sure it's done. A pork butt at 170° and one at 190° look and feel very similar. This will most likely take between 7 and 10 hours depending on your grill, the size of your pork butt, and the exact temperature. I've had it take up to 14 hours on a finicky charcoal grill.

7. When the pork hits the desired temperature, remove it from the grill and wrap tightly in foil. Let it rest for 30 minutes.

8. Shred the pork with two forks and use it in sandwiches, or store it for use in other recipes. It will store well in the fridge for 7 days. If you're freezing it for later, I recommend dividing it into 1-pound servings and freezing it in freezer-safe storage bags.

Slow Cooker Pork Butt

. . . .

This is a very different end product from the grilled pork butt. Both recipes will result in pulled pork, but this version is cooked in a liquid. It's basically braised for hours and hours. It gets a lot of its flavor from the liquid, while the grilled version gets its flavor from a rub and the natural fats in the pork.

Have no fear, though; you can still use this pulled pork in all the supporting recipes. Just be sure to follow the step about removing all the liquid from the slow cooker and adding only a part of it back in, so your pork isn't too soupy.

For my money, if I have the time I usually grill my pork butt low and slow, but who has the time to spend a day doing that regularly? You can make this recipe while you are at work!

Servings: about 6 pounds pulled pork, enough for about 30 sandwiches or 10–12 cups shredded pork | Prep Time: 15 minutes | Total Time: 10 hours

8-pound pork butt (aka shoulder)

1 large onion, grated

1 (12-ounce) beer (any good lager works)

½ cup brown sugar

1 (6-ounce) can tomato paste

¼ cup soy sauce

1 large cinnamon stick

2 tablespoons paprika

1 tablespoon chili powder

1 tablespoon kosher salt

1 tablespoon black pepper

1. Cut pork butt into four or five large pieces so it fits in your slow cooker. Cut off any large pieces of fat from it. You don't need that much fat since the pork is cooking in liquid.

2. Mix together all the other ingredients in the slow cooker so they are well combined. Add pork pieces to the liquid, cover, and cook on low for 8 to 10 hours.

3. Remove pork pieces and let them cool for a few minutes. Pour liquid into a bowl.

4. Shred pork pieces using two forks. Try to remove any huge pieces of fat from the pork. The pork should shred very easily. Return shredded pork to dry slow cooker.

5. Pour cooking liquid back into slow cooker in 1-cup increments until the pork is moist, but not soupy at all. I think 2 to 3 cups of liquid is about right, but feel free to add more or less to taste. Just remember that if your pork is too wet, it will make your buns soggy later.

6. Keep the pulled pork warm while serving. Serve with toasted buns, barbecue sauce, and coleslaw for a classic meal.

7. Store leftovers in the fridge for up to a week, or freeze leftovers in an airtight, freezer-safe container for up to a few months.

Leftover Liquid

After you've cooked the pork, pulled it, and added some of the cooking liquid back to the slow cooker, you will most likely still have a few cups of cooking liquid. This liquid has great flavor and can be used in lots of ways. To make a really simple sauce, just add 2 cups of it to a medium pot and simmer for 20 minutes until it reduces and thickens. Season the sauce with a squirt of ketchup, a dash of vinegar, and some salt and pepper.

Optionally, you can also add up to a cup of the liquid to the Honey Bourbon BBQ Sauce recipe in this chapter, which will require simmering the sauce for an extra 5 to 10 minutes to thicken it, but it will make the flavor more complex.

Honey Bourbon BBQ Sauce

There are a ton of barbecue sauces in most supermarkets these days, so one might ask why any sane person would make their own. I'll be completely honest, I'm not sure that I have the best answer to that question. Some store-bought versions do have a lot of sugar and preservatives, but you can find good ones also. All I know is that I love my homemade version, and it doesn't take that long to make. If you have a store-bought version that you like, go with it. If you feel like getting frisky, here's one of my favorite homemade versions.

Servings: Makes about 2½ cups sauce | Prep Time: 10 minutes | Total Time: 45 minutes

1 medium white onion

¼ cup vegetable or canola oil

¼ cup butter

1–2 Serrano peppers, minced

1 cup bourbon

½ cup ketchup

¾ cup apple cider vinegar

¼ cup molasses

¼ cup honey

¼ cup Worcestershire sauce

Salt

1. Grate onion so it almost dissolves in the final sauce. I use one medium onion, which measures about a cup. It doesn't have to be exact (don't pull out a second onion for an extra few tablespoons).

2. Add oil and butter to a medium pot over medium heat. Once butter is melted, add onion and minced pepper. Cook until onion is soft, but not browned, about 4 to 5 minutes.

3. Add bourbon, ketchup, vinegar, molasses, honey, and Worcestershire to the pan and stir well to combine. Bring sauce to a slow simmer and cook until it nearly halves in volume, about 25 minutes.

4. Taste the sauce and season with salt.

5. Serve immediately or store in the fridge until needed. Sauce will keep for 2 weeks in the fridge.

Sriracha Slaw

Whether you cook your pulled pork on the grill, in the oven, or in a slow cooker, coleslaw is a classic side dish. The tangy flavor and crunchy texture pair well with rich meat. Store-bought coleslaw tends to be a disaster in my opinion. It normally resembles mayonnaise soup. This recipe has just enough dressing to coat the slaw and gets a nice punch of heat from some Sriracha chili sauce.

Servings: 8 | Prep Time: 10 minutes | Total Time: 15 minutes

1. Stir the mayonnaise, vinegar, and chili sauce together in a large bowl. Add scallions and season with salt and pepper. Stir well to combine.

2. Toss cabbage mix into bowl and stir to coat well. Feel free to use your hands!

3. This recipe is best if you allow it to sit in the fridge for at least a few hours. Then taste for salt and pepper; it might need another pinch of both. Store in the fridge until needed!

½ cup mayonnaise

¼ cup apple cider vinegar

2–3 tablespoons Sriracha chili sauce

3 scallions, minced

¾ teaspoon kosher salt

¾ teaspoon black pepper

16 ounces shredded cabbage mix

Carnitas Tacos

These are traditional tacos. That means they aren't slathered in gooey cheese and overloaded with stuff like lettuce, tomatoes, and sour cream. The focus of these tacos is the pork—as it should be. There are a few basic, traditional toppings, but none of them overpower the delicious pork flavors.

I prefer corn tortillas for these guys, but flour tortillas are okay too. If you're feeling frisky, light up your gas grill or gas burners on your stove and toast the tortillas for a few seconds per side directly over the flame. Just flip them with some tongs and get a light sear on the tortillas. That makes for one amazing taco.

Servings: 8 tacos | Prep Time: 15 minutes | Total Time: 45 minutes

Quick Pickled Red Onion

1 red onion

1 large lime, juice only

½ teaspoon kosher salt

1 pound (about 3 cups) shredded pork

3 tablespoons unsalted butter, melted

16 (6-inch) corn tortillas (or 8 flour tortillas)

2 avocados, mashed

4 radishes, sliced thin

Fresh cilantro

1 lime, juice only

1. Preheat oven to 425°F.

2. **For pickled red onions:** Peel onion and slice it first in half and then into thin slivers. Add to a bowl and toss with lime juice and salt. Let sit at room temperature for at least 15 minutes while you make the rest of the carnitas.

3. Add shredded pork to an 8 x 8-inch baking dish. Try to spread out pork so it is in a thin layer covering the entire pan. Drizzle pork with melted butter.

4. Bake until the shredded pork becomes crispy on top, 10 to 12 minutes.

5. Meanwhile, prepare your other toppings.

6. **For the tortillas:** If you have a gas range, you can toast the corn tortillas directly over the gas flame over medium heat, but make sure your cooking surface is very clean. Let the tortillas cook

until they are lightly charred, about 10 seconds per side. Otherwise, toast them in a dry skillet over medium-high heat for about 30 seconds per side.

7. **To make tacos:** Use two toasted corn tortillas per taco, or one flour tortilla. Smear tortillas with some mashed avocado. Pile on a scoop of baked carnitas followed by sliced radishes, fresh cilantro, pickled red onions, and a squeeze of fresh lime juice.

Pulled Pork BBQ Pizza

I've always tried to be an honest person, so I'll tell you that the first time I ate this pizza, I had consumed more than one adult beverage. That's all you need to know. I thought it was a delicious creation, but the next day I was a bit concerned that I only thought it was delicious because of, well, the beer.

In a sober light, I was happy to discover that it was still delicious. There are only a few ingredients, but don't skip any of them. They all bring something wonderful to the pizza.

Servings: 4, or 2 medium pizzas | Prep Time: 15 minutes plus pizza dough prep | Total Time: 30 minutes

2 (8-ounce) pizza dough balls (see Napoletano Pizza Dough on page 77 or use store-bought)

Cornmeal, for pizza peel

½ cup barbecue sauce

10 ounces (about 2½ cups) grated mozzarella cheese

4 ounces (about 1 cup) grated smoked Gouda cheese

10 ounces (1½–2 cups) shredded pork

½ red onion, sliced thin

Salt and pepper

Red pepper flakes (optional)

Cilantro

1. If you are using homemade dough, be sure to take it out of the fridge at least an hour before rolling it.

2. Preheat oven to 500°F with pizza stone in oven for 20 minutes.

3. Roll dough out on a lightly floured surface into a thin disk. Stretch the dough carefully with your hands until it reaches the desired size, 10 to 12 inches in diameter.

4. Dust a pizza peel with cornmeal and place dough on peel.

5. Spread ¼ cup barbecue sauce onto dough, leaving about ⅓ inch around the edges.

6. Top pizza with 5 ounces mozzarella cheese and 2 ounces smoked Gouda. Add a scant cup of shredded pork and sliced red onions, distributed evenly over the pizza. Season pizza with a pinch of salt and pepper and optional red pepper flakes.

7. Slide pizza onto the hot pizza stone and bake until the crust is nicely browned and the center is bubbly, 11 to 12 minutes.

8. Remove pizza carefully with peel and let cool for a minute before slicing.

9. Garnish pizzas with freshly chopped cilantro.

10. Serve immediately! Unlike most pizza, this one isn't great cold because cold pork isn't the best. If you need to reheat it, do so in a 350°F oven for a few minutes to keep the crust crispy.

Banh Mi

Banh mi is a traditional Vietnamese sandwich that features some sort of roasted meat (usually pork) and lots of fresh and pickled vegetables. It almost always has some type of spicy sauce. My wife is a huge banh mi fan and usually wants just the traditional version. Don't fix what isn't broken, right? She gave this version two thumbs up even though I made some substitutions. These substitutions are necessary unless you want to start your own pickling production line just to make a freakin' sandwich. The key to this sandwich is chopping up the pork and simmering it for a few minutes in the sauce. It makes the pork extra tender and gives it loads of flavor. Trust me on the fish sauce. It makes everything click.

Servings: 2 sandwiches | Prep Time: 15 minutes | Total Time: 30 minutes

1. Preheat oven to 400°F.

2. One baguette should get you two large sandwiches. If you can't find a baguette the appropriate length, just get a larger one and cut it to size. Slice baguette down the center and toast in oven until it's lightly crispy, about 5 minutes, while you prepare the other ingredients.

3. In a medium saucepan, add oil over medium heat. Once hot, add minced garlic and cook for a minute until soft.

4. Roughly chop the pulled pork and add it to the pan. Add fish sauce, water, sugar, and black pepper. Simmer the pork in the mixture until it is soft and all the liquid is absorbed, 3 to 4 minutes.

5. Whisk mayonnaise and Sriracha chili sauce in a small bowl. Feel free to add more hot sauce to suit your taste.

6. Slather both sides of toasted bread with the mayo. Pile the cooked pork onto the bottom piece of bread and top with fresh and pickled vegetables.

7. Garnish sandwich with fresh cilantro leaves and an extra drizzle of Sriracha if that's your thing. Top the sandwich and cut it in half to make it easier to eat.

1 large baguette, 14–16 inches long

1 teaspoon vegetable or olive oil

1 clove garlic, minced

10 ounces (1½–2 cups) pulled pork

1 tablespoon fish sauce

¼ cup water

Pinch of sugar

Pinch of black pepper

Quick Sriracha Mayonnaise

⅓ cup mayonnaise

1 tablespoon Sriracha chili sauce

½ cucumber, sliced thin

1 small carrot, grated

1 small daikon radish, grated

1 red jalapeño, sliced thin

Pickled banana peppers

Fresh cilantro, garnish

Sriracha chili sauce

Pork Polenta Pie

This is one of those meals that pays large dividends of your time and leftovers. The polenta layers might look complicated, but they are actually straightforward, and the pork filling is warming and delicious. It has one of the longer total times for a dish in this book, but I thought it was good enough to include. It also feeds an army!

Servings: 8 | Prep Time: 45 minutes | Total Time: 1 hour 45 minutes

Basic Polenta

6 cups water

¾ teaspoon kosher salt

½ teaspoon ground pepper

2 cups coarse polenta

Filling

2 tablespoons olive oil

1 cup minced leek or white onion

½ cup minced carrots

1 stalk celery, minced

2 cloves garlic, minced

1 teaspoon ground fennel seeds

½ teaspoon red pepper flakes

Pinch of salt and pepper

¼ cup tomato paste

½ cup red wine

1 (28-ounce) can diced tomatoes

1 pound (about 3 cups) pulled pork

2 tablespoons minced fresh oregano

1 tablespoon minced fresh thyme

8 ounces semi-firm cheese, like Gouda

Fresh parsley, garnish

1. **For the polenta:** Line a 11 x 16-inch sheet pan with plastic wrap.

2. In a large pot, bring 6 cups of water to a simmer and add salt and pepper.

3. Once simmering, whisk in polenta and continue to stir until very thick, about 5 minutes.

Note: You should check the directions for your specific polenta brand, but most call for a 3–1 water-to-polenta ratio.

4. Once thick, immediately pour polenta onto sheet pan and spread evenly over pan. Let cool until firm, about 20 to 30 minutes.

5. **To make the pie:** Preheat oven to 350°F.

6. In a large pot, add oil over medium heat. Once hot, add in leeks, carrots, celery, and garlic and cook until vegetables soften, about 5 minutes. Add in ground fennel seeds, red pepper flakes, and a pinch of salt and pepper.

7. Add tomato paste to pan and stir until paste coats the vegetables. Then add red wine followed by diced tomatoes. Bring to a simmer and cook mixture for about 5 minutes.

8. Meanwhile, dice leftover pulled pork finely. It should almost resemble ground pork. Add pork and fresh oregano and thyme to filling ingredients and stir well to combine. Let simmer on low heat for 15 minutes, stirring regularly. Taste for salt and pepper. You might need a pinch of both.

9. When you're ready to make the polenta pie, cut the polenta into squares and peel the firm pieces off the baking sheet. The plastic wrap should help with removal. Line the bottom of a 9 x 13-inch baking dish with half of the polenta pieces. It's okay if the polenta doesn't go all the way to the edges of the pan.

10. Spoon half of the pork filling over the polenta and then sprinkle with half of the grated cheese. Repeat with another layer of polenta squares and the rest of the pork filling and cheese. The final pie should be pretty thick.

11. Bake dish until the cheese is melted and bubbling, about 45 minutes.

12. Let cool for 5 minutes before serving. Garnish each serving with chopped parsley.

Pulled Pork Mac-n-Cheese

Macaroni and cheese is pretty hard to screw up, but I did actually have to try out a few versions of this recipe before I learned that keeping it simple is best. You don't need or want a bunch of crazy add-ins. Start with a really good homemade cheese sauce and add in some barbecue sauce for sweetness. The pork then ties everything together!

Servings: 8 | Prep Time: 15 minutes | Total Time: 40 minutes

1. Preheat oven to 375°F.

2. Cook macaroni pasta according to package. Be sure not to overcook the pasta or you'll end up with mushy macaroni and cheese. Drain pasta and set aside for later.

3. In a large pot, add unsalted butter and flour over medium heat. Whisk together as butter melts.

4. Continue to cook until the mixture forms a thick paste (a roux). Cook the roux, whisking occasionally, until the mixture turns a light tan color, 2 to 3 minutes. If your roux is more liquid, that's fine as long as it's the right color. A paste is best though.

5. Slowly start whisking in warm milk. The sauce should thicken immediately. Work in about 1-cup batches, and let the sauce heat up and thicken in between batches. Once all the milk is added, the sauce might look a bit thin, but that's okay.

6. Add grated gruyère and cheddar and stir well to melt cheese. Add barbecue sauce and season with salt and pepper.

7. Stir cooked macaroni into the sauce. Pour macaroni into a 9 x 13-inch baking dish and top with chopped pulled pork.

8. Move dish to oven and bake for 15 minutes, uncovered, to crisp up the pork pieces. Serve immediately!

Ingredients:

1 pound macaroni pasta

¼ cup unsalted butter

¼ cup all-purpose flour

3 cups warm milk

8 ounces gruyère cheese, grated

8 ounces sharp cheddar cheese, grated

⅓ cup barbecue sauce

Salt and pepper

1 pound (about 3 cups) chopped pulled pork

Note: You can easily halve this recipe; if you do so, use an 8 x 8-inch baking dish.

El Cubano

This sandwich is traditionally made on a grill and pressed down with a brick or heavy sandwich press. This is hard to replicate at home unless you happen to have a heavy brick sitting around!

    I solve the problem by baking the sandwich in a hot oven with a very hot cast-iron skillet resting on top of the sandwich. As the sandwich bakes, the hot, heavy skillet presses it down and gets the job done. If you happen to have a panini press, you could use that as well.

Servings: 2 | Prep Time: 10 minutes | Total Time: 30 minutes

1 large baguette or medium French loaf

Dijon mustard

¼ pound Swiss cheese, sliced

Sliced pickles

⅓ pound (about a cup) smoked ham

⅓ pound (about a cup) chopped pulled pork

1. Preheat oven to 400°F. Heat a large cast-iron skillet in the oven.

2. Slice baguette in half down the middle. Slather both sides of the bread with Dijon mustard.

3. Add a few slices of Swiss cheese to the bottom piece of bread and lay on a few pickle slices. Add sliced ham to the sandwich followed by the chopped pulled pork.

4. Add the top piece of bread to the sandwich and set it on a baking sheet. Lay a piece of foil on top of the sandwich.

5. When the oven is hot, carefully remove the cast-iron skillet and place it on top of the sandwich so foil is in between skillet and sandwich. It should balance without too much problem. This will press the sandwich as it cooks.

6. Carefully place the baking sheet, sandwich, and skillet all back into the oven. Bake for 10 to 12 minutes.

7. Remove baking sheet and carefully remove skillet from the top. Cut sandwich in half and serve immediately!

Snap Pea and Pork Stir-Fry

Stir-fry is the quintessential leftover dish. You can toss in almost anything, and if your sauce is good (this one is), then you'll be in fine shape. I highly recommend following this recipe as-is because the veggies included here work really well with the lightly fried pork pieces, but I won't tell anyone if you substitute some of the veggies for ones you happen to have on hand.

Servings: 4 | Prep Time: 20 minutes | Total Time: 45 minutes

1. Whisk together all the ingredients for the sauce. Set aside.

2. Break or cut off hard ends from asparagus and chop into 1-inch-long pieces. Mince the ginger, shallots, and garlic finely and set aside.

3. If you're using pulled pork from the slow cooker recipe, drain off as much liquid as possible from the pork before making this recipe. You want to start with fairly dry pulled pork.

4. Bring a large pot of water to boil and season well with kosher salt (about 1 tablespoon per gallon of water). Once boiling, add the asparagus and snap peas and cook for 60 seconds. Drain and rinse vegetables under cold water to stop the cooking.

5. Heat a large wok or skillet over high heat. Once hot, add oil followed by chopped pork. Cook pork over high heat until it starts to turn crispy, about 5 minutes.

6. Add diced red peppers and continue to cook for another 2 to 3 minutes.

7. Add garlic, shallot, and ginger to wok and cook for another minute, stirring constantly to make sure these ingredients don't burn.

8. Add sauce to the pan and toss to combine. Let sauce reduce for about 30 seconds.

9. Finally, add blanched vegetables and toss to combine. Serve stir-fry immediately over rice.

Stir-Fry Sauce

¼ cup soy sauce

¼ cup water

2 tablespoons rice wine vinegar

2 tablespoons fish sauce

1 tablespoon brown sugar

1 teaspoon cornstarch

½ teaspoon red pepper flakes

1 bunch thin asparagus

1 3-inch piece fresh ginger

2 large shallots

2 cloves garlic

1 pound (about 3 cups) chopped pulled pork

Kosher salt

2 cups sugar snap peas

3 tablespoons vegetable oil

1 red pepper, diced

Cooked rice for serving

CHAPTER 10
GRILLED TOFU

If I had to pick out a dorky kid of the food world, it would probably be tofu. It's usually by itself in the grocery store, pushed way back on a dim shelf, neglected and alone. People are always taking cheap shots at it and laughing behind its back.

Much like how the dorky kid in school always grows up to be a millionaire model superhero (or food blogger in some cases), tofu is finally having its moment in the sun. People are starting to appreciate that it's not only for vegetarians. They are beginning to realize that, bang for the buck, it's one of the most versatile things you can buy in the grocery store. Maybe most important, people now recognize that it can be delicious.

The first time you buy tofu, it can be intimidating. For starters, there are various firmness levels that are unique to tofu. Generally, at a minimum you'll find soft or silken, firm, and extra-firm tofu. Can you imagine walking through the poultry section and seeing silken, firm, and extra-firm chicken? Confusing, right?

Then, assuming you muster up the courage to buy a square of the stuff, you get home to find that it's immersed in some sort of briny liquid, bland as all get out, and seemingly about as useful as a piece of soaked cardboard.

Stay with me though. If you can spend a few minutes with this strange drowned block of food, you can transform it into some really incredible meals throughout the week. As with all the main dishes in this book, tofu keeps amazingly well. In fact, it might just win the award for storage. Also, once you get a few tofu tests under your belt, I think you'll find that it's at least as easy to cook as any meat item in your fridge.

I sincerely encourage even the heartiest of carnivores to give this dorky kid a second shot. I think you'll fall in love.

There are two major battles when preparing tofu. First, unless you're making something like a smoothie or a soup, you'll want to improve its texture. Tofu is best when it is crispy on the outside, and that can be a hard texture to achieve when you purchase it submerged in water. Second, you'll want to give it some flavor. Tofu is notorious for being bland, so it's okay to load it up with flavors.

Tofu is used a lot in stir-fries but I think it's easiest to grill. You can marinate it in various flavors, and a hot grill pretty much guarantees a good texture.

Pressing Concerns

Unless you are using your tofu in something liquid, it's always a good idea to press it to squeeze out as much of the liquid as possible. To do this, lay a few paper towels on a clean surface and then place your block or blocks of tofu on top of them. I recommend slicing your tofu blocks in half longwise to speed up the pressing process. Add another layer of paper towels on top of the tofu slices and then place something flat on top of the tofu. Set a weight or something heavy on top of the flat surface (I use a large bowl filled with water). Then let it sit for about 20 minutes.

You'll find that the paper towels are completely soaked with liquid and the tofu blocks are a bit lighter and a bit dryer. As an experiment, I weighed my tofu before and after pressing it and found that the blocks went from 16 ounces to 13 ounces. In other words, a little less than 20 percent of the weight of the tofu was just water that is better out than in!

Even if you are pressed for time, find the time to press your tofu.

Grilled Sesame Tofu

There are more ways to cook tofu than ways to cook a steak, but the key to cooking tofu correctly almost always involves really high heat. For my money, grilling it is easiest. The other benefit of grilling tofu is that you can grill a ton at a time, which means you can make enough tofu in one batch for a whole week of meals.

This grilled tofu is fantastic as a meal served with rice and steamed veggies, but you can also use it right away in many of the supporting recipes in this chapter. Once the grilled tofu has cooled down, store it in an airtight container or plastic bag in the fridge for seven to ten days.

Servings: 4, but easily doubled | Prep Time: 45 minutes, including pressing time and marinating time | Total Time: 1 hour

2 (16-ounce) blocks firm or extra-firm tofu

¼ cup soy sauce

2 tablespoons sesame oil

1 tablespoon Sriracha chili sauce (optional)

1. Drain blocks of tofu and slice them in half longwise. Lay out a few paper towels on a clean surface. Lay tofu blocks on top of paper towels and top with another layer of paper towels. Add something flat to the top like a large cutting board and then place some weight on top to press the tofu. I like to use a large mixing bowl filled with water. Let the tofu press for 20 minutes.

2. Whisk together soy sauce, sesame oil, and chili sauce in a bowl.

3. When tofu is done pressing, add to marinade and let sit at room temperature for 15 to 20 minutes. Alternatively, you could let this marinate overnight in the fridge.

4. Heat grill to high heat while tofu marinates. If you don't have access to a grill, you can also use a grill pan over the stove on medium-high heat.

5. Once tofu is done marinating, add to hot grill and grill until nicely seared on both sides, 4 to 5 minutes per side. If you're using a grill pan, you might need to cook it for a few extra minutes.

Note: Feel free to expand on the marinade for this recipe. I used a basic marinade that has only three ingredients but packs in the flavor. You could add in some minced garlic, ginger, or chiles to give the marinade extra flavor.

Note: Tofu is typically sold in both 14-ounce and 16-ounce containers. Either size will work for this recipe.

Tofu Smoothie

In the summer months this is the go-to breakfast in our house. You might think that a smoothie isn't substantial enough to get you through the day, but the tofu adds lots of protein, and the jumbo serving makes it filling.

This is the one recipe in this chapter that doesn't work with the grilled tofu recipe. You can use any firmness of tofu for this smoothie, but definitely don't use cooked tofu. Reserve a block of it uncooked to toss into this quick breakfast.

Servings: 2 large smoothies | Prep Time: 10 minutes | Total Time: 10 minutes

1 cup orange or apple juice

½ **cup tofu**

½ **cup yogurt**

1 banana

2 cups assorted frozen fruit (raspberries, strawberries, blueberries)

¼ **cup ground flaxseed (optional)**

2 tablespoons chia seeds (optional)

Add all the ingredients to a blender. I recommend adding the frozen fruit last. That seems to make it blend easier. Blend until smooth and serve immediately!

Tofu Frittata

I would never really think to put raw tofu in a frittata. It would just turn into a mushy mess. Leftover grilled tofu, however, becomes a great addition. This frittata is a perfect brunch dish and will actually keep decently in the fridge for a few days if you can't get through it all right away.

Servings: 8 slices | Prep Time: 15 minutes | Total Time: 45 minutes

1. Preheat oven to 350°F.

2. Whisk together eggs and milk and set aside until needed.

3. Heat a large, heavy, oven-safe skillet (12-inch cast-iron works well) over medium heat. Once skillet is hot, add olive oil and onions. Cook onions until they start to soften, about 4 to 5 minutes.

4. Add thinly sliced chard, the Serrano pepper, cooked tofu, and garlic and stir well. Continue to cook for another minute to lightly wilt greens.

5. Add lemon juice. Make sure ingredients are evenly spread around the pan. Then sprinkle ingredients with cheese and immediately pour in the scrambled eggs.

6. Season the dish with salt and pepper and transfer it to the oven. Bake until eggs are firm, about 15 minutes.

7. Remove frittata and sprinkle with minced fresh oregano. Serve immediately with a sprinkle of salt and pepper and hot sauce on the side.

8 large eggs

¼ cup milk

2 tablespoons olive oil

1 cup diced white or yellow onions

2 cups thinly sliced Swiss chard

1 Serrano pepper, minced

6 ounces (a heaping cup) grilled tofu, cubed

2 cloves garlic, minced

½ lemon, juice only

1 cup grated cheddar or Pepper Jack cheese

Salt and pepper

2 teaspoons minced fresh oregano, garnish

Spicy Soba Soup

I originally intended this soup to be a sort of appetizer, but it can easily work as a main course soup. In fact, on a cold day a big bowl of this soup is all I need. It has light flavors in it but is really filling thanks to the soba and tofu. There are some spicy elements in the soup base, but I recommend dashing some hot sauce into it as well before digging in.

While I wrote this recipe to use cooked tofu, you can just press and cube uncooked tofu and toss it in. It will absorb flavor from the broth and be great.

Servings: 4 large bowls of soup | Prep Time: 15 minutes | Total Time: 30 minutes

1. Add stock and water to a large pot. Add in the sliced ginger (no need to peel it), crushed garlic cloves, and dried chile peppers. Bring the soup base to a simmer over high heat, then reduce heat to low, cover, and simmer for 20 minutes.

2. While soup base simmers, cook soba according to package instructions. Do not cook the soba in the soup base because the noodles will really thicken it. Once soba is cooked through, drain and rinse with cold water to stop the cooking. Then toss the noodles with a few tablespoons of sesame oil so they don't stick together.

3. Once the soup base has simmered, remove the ginger, garlic, and chili peppers. Add the tofu cubes and edamame to the base and simmer for another 5 minutes.

4. Divide soba noodles between four bowls and ladle soup over the top of the noodles, ensuring that you get plenty of edamame and tofu in each bowl.

5. Garnish each bowl with chopped scallions and serve with soy sauce and chili sauce.

1 quart low-sodium vegetable stock

1 quart water

4 inches fresh ginger, sliced

6 cloves garlic, crushed whole

4 dried arbol or bird chile peppers (optional)

8 ounces soba noodles

2 tablespoons toasted sesame oil

8 ounces (1½ cups) grilled or uncooked tofu, cubed

2 cups frozen shelled edamame

4 chopped scallions, garnish

Soy sauce

Sriracha chili sauce

Sesame Salad

I try to eat at least one salad a day on average. Most of the time I'll make a small side salad for dinner, but occasionally I will have a big salad for lunch. This salad works great either way. It's one of the most unique salads I've made in the last year or so. I'm particularly proud of the nori croutons, but you could leave them out if you can't easily find the nori sushi papers.

Servings: 2–4 salads | Prep Time: 15 minutes | Total Time: 15 minutes

Sesame Dressing

2 tablespoons soy sauce

2 tablespoons rice wine vinegar

2 tablespoons grapeseed or peanut oil

2 tablespoons toasted sesame oil

2 tablespoons honey

Dash of hot sauce

¼ cup mixed sesame seeds (white and black if possible)

2 sheets nori paper

1 head green leaf lettuce, chopped

1 large cucumber, diced

1 cup shredded carrots

1 cup sliced daikon radish

½ cup sprouts

6–8 ounces (1–1½ cups) cooked tofu, cubed

1. In a medium bowl, whisk together dressing ingredients. Taste dressing and adjust flavors to your liking. It's possible you might want to add more vinegar, honey, or soy sauce to suit your taste.

2. Add sesame seeds to a dry skillet over low heat and toast until they are fragrant, about 4 to 5 minutes. Keep a close eye on the seeds and stir them regularly, as they will burn quickly.

3. Remove seeds from skillet and add nori paper to the dry skillet. Again, toast over low heat until the nori paper starts to curl. This should take just a minute or two. Remove quickly so it doesn't burn and roughly chop toasted nori paper to make croutons.

4. Arrange chopped lettuce on plates and top with cucumber, carrots, daikon radish, sprouts, and tofu. Drizzle salad with a small amount of sesame dressing and serve the rest on the side.

5. Garnish each salad with toasted nori croutons and sesame seeds.

Asian Salad Wraps

I can pretty much guarantee that these will be one of the healthiest things you eat all week. You will also find yourself wanting to smack others who try to steal your salad wraps. It's not that they are hard to make or anything, but they are *yours.*

While I call these wraps, they are actually almost impossible to wrap up like a burrito. The lettuce will likely be too crispy to do that. You should be able to fold them up so you can hold them like a taco and eat them though. Make sure you have plenty of napkins on hand.

Servings: 4 wraps | Prep Time: 15 minutes | Total Time: 15 minutes

1. Whisk together soy sauce, lime juice, and red pepper flakes to make a quick dipping sauce for the wraps.

2. Rinse four large romaine lettuce leaves and pat them dry.

3. Slice the avocado and divide it evenly between the four lettuce leaves.

4. Divide tofu evenly between the wraps and top with red peppers, carrots, and sprouts. Garnish with a few fresh cilantro leaves.

5. As you eat each wrap like a taco, spoon a bit of the sauce over the top of it.

Dipping Sauce
3 tablespoons soy sauce
½ lime, juice only
¼ teaspoon red pepper flakes

4 large romaine lettuce leaves
1 avocado
2–3 ounces (½ cup) cooked tofu, sliced thin
½ red pepper, sliced thin
¼ cup shredded carrot
¼ cup sprouts
Fresh cilantro, garnish

Tofu and Eggplant Stir-Fry

Eggplant isn't a hugely popular stir-fry ingredient, but I think it gives some great texture to this dish. If you aren't familiar with cooking eggplant, the larger ones can be kind of bitter, so I recommend using smaller ones for this dish. By smaller, I mean that two to three eggplants should equal a pound by weight. If you can only find the big guys, no big deal, just follow the directions below and lightly salt the eggplant. Salting it will press out some of the bitterness. It will add about half an hour onto your prep time though.

Servings: 6 | Prep Time: 25 minutes | Total Time: 45 minutes

1 pound small eggplants

3 tablespoons peanut or vegetable oil, divided

1 red pepper, diced

4 cloves garlic, minced

2 inches fresh ginger, grated

10–14 ounces (2–2½ cups) cooked tofu, cubed

Sauce

2 tablespoons soy sauce

1 tablespoon fish sauce

½ lime, juice only

1 tablespoon brown sugar

1 tablespoon Sriracha chili sauce

1 tablespoon rice wine vinegar

¼ cup chopped fresh basil, garnish

4 scallions, chopped, garnish

Cooked rice for serving

1. If you can find smaller eggplants (two to three per pound), chop them into 1-inch cubes. (If you can find only large eggplants, slice the eggplant into 1-inch slices and line the inside of a colander with the slices. Sprinkle slices with ½ teaspoon kosher salt. Continue to layer eggplant and salt, then top the eggplant with a bowl that fits inside the colander. Fill the bowl partially with water. Let eggplant press for 30 minutes, then rinse with cold water and dry. Cut the slices into 1-inch pieces.)

2. Once your eggplant is ready, add 2 tablespoons oil to a large skillet or wok over high heat. Add eggplant and cook until browned, about 8 minutes, stirring occasionally. If the pan is very dry at any point, add more oil.

3. Remove eggplant and add red pepper, garlic, and ginger to the pan. If pan is very dry, add another tablespoon oil. Cook for a minute until veggies soften.

4. Add eggplant back to pan along with cubed tofu.

5. In a small bowl, mix together all ingredients for sauce, then pour sauce into pan and stir everything together. Cook until sauce thickens, another minute or two.

6. Garnish stir-fry with fresh basil and scallions. Serve over rice.

Black Pepper Tofu

I've included two stir-fry dishes in the same chapter! I just couldn't leave out this dish, because if you are pressed for time and want something spicy and filling, this is about as good as it gets. In less than thirty minutes, you can have this dish on the table—and it packs a ton of flavor. You might think that the amount of black pepper listed is a typo when you measure it. I assure you it is not. Just go with it.

Servings: 4 | Prep Time: 15 minutes | Total Time: 30 minutes

Sauce

3 tablespoons soy sauce

1 tablespoon sugar

1 tablespoon sesame oil

4 tablespoons unsalted butter

½ cup (about 3 large) minced shallot

2 red jalapeños, diced with seeds

5 cloves garlic, minced

2 inches fresh ginger, minced

1 tablespoon black peppercorns

14 ounces (2½ cups) cooked tofu, cubed

6 scallions, chopped, garnish

Cooked rice for serving

1. In a small bowl, whisk together soy sauce, sugar, and sesame oil for the sauce and set aside.

2. Add butter to a wok or large skillet and once melted, add shallot, red jalapeños, garlic, and ginger. Cook over medium-high heat until veggies start to soften, about 3 to 4 minutes. Stir constantly to prevent burning.

3. Grind peppercorns roughly.

4. Pour soy sauce mixture into wok and immediately add black pepper and tofu. Toss to combine and heat tofu. Let cook for a minute to thicken sauce.

5. Garnish with chopped scallions and serve immediately with rice.

Tofu Veggie Stack

This is a lighter dish and works well for lunch. If you want to eat it as a full dinner, you could easily serve it over a starch like rice or pasta.

This dish works best if you have some in-season squash or zucchini, because it stacks easily and pairs well with the other flavors. If you can't find squash, you can use only mushrooms instead and double the amount.

Servings: 2 stacks | Prep Time: 15 minutes | Total Time: 40 minutes

1. **To make the quick pesto:** Add all the ingredients to a small food processor and process until smooth. Feel free to add a bit more olive oil if the pesto is too thick.

2. Lay sliced tofu in a baking dish. Heat oven to 250°F. Let tofu warm in the oven as you cook the rest of the ingredients.

3. Add 2 tablespoons butter or olive oil to a large skillet over medium heat. Once hot, add sliced mushrooms and cook until mushrooms release their liquid and soften, about 6 to 8 minutes. Season with a pinch of salt and pepper and remove mushrooms.

4. If pan is dry, add a drizzle of oil. Lay squash or zucchini slices in the skillet and cook for about 3 to 4 minutes per side over medium-high heat. The slices should soften and brown slightly.

5. To make the stack, divide the cooked mushrooms between two plates. Top each stack of mushrooms with a slice or two of tofu, followed by half the squash or zucchini on each plate. Top with the rest of the warmed tofu and drizzle the whole stack with pesto. Serve immediately!

Quick Pesto
1 cup fresh basil
¼ cup olive oil
1 clove garlic
¼ cup Parmesan cheese

6–8 ounces (1 heaping cup) cooked tofu, sliced longwise
2 tablespoons unsalted butter or olive oil
8 ounces cremini mushrooms, sliced
Salt and pepper
1 medium squash or zucchini, sliced longwise

CHAPTER 11
GRANOLA

One of the more popular series of posts on my blog is called "The Home-made Trials." Basically, I pick a food item like macaroni and cheese or pudding and then compare a homemade version to a bunch of different store-bought varieties. I completely geek out on these and compare the varieties not only on how delicious they are, but also on how long they take to prepare, how much they cost, and how nutritious they are.

Sometimes I'm pretty surprised by the results in *both* directions. Foods that I think would be clearly in the "buy" category work out to be better if you make them from scratch and vice-versa. A while back I ran granola through The Homemade Trials and came out with a pretty close result.

While you can definitely buy decent granola these days, it tends to be more expensive than if you buy the bulk individual ingredients. This is true even if you are using really expensive ingredients like walnuts, dates, honey, and good vanilla.

From a nutritional standpoint, I found granola to be pretty similar across the board unless you are doing something crazy like mixing it with lots of booze and mascarpone cheese (like I do in my Granola Tiramisu recipe on page 183). That obviously changes the calculus a bit. But most granola is pretty healthy and a great way to start the day. Without a doubt I think granola is healthier than most cereals on the market, which tend to be super sugar-packed.

The other nice characteristic about granola is that it has a great shelf life. If you store it in an airtight container, it'll keep for weeks without a problem. This makes it a fantastic base recipe for leftovers. While the base recipe in this chapter makes a decent amount of granola, you could easily double it and be set for a long time.

Of course, you don't have to always make it yourself. If you find a brand and type that you like, then you can certainly use that granola for the supporting recipes in this chapter.

If you're looking to save a few bucks, or if you want to try some new flavors, give homemade granola a shot. It takes less than an hour to make a huge batch. It can be a bit intimidating once you realize that you can put almost anything in granola, but that's half the fun of it!

Baked Granola

It's really hard to go wrong with granola, but it can be intimidating if you're just sitting there staring at oats and a huge wall of possible add-ins. This basic recipe is a starting point. It's simple and has just a few important ingredients. Of course, you can adjust all the add-ins to your liking, but I think you'll find this version to be a good base.

As you will see, there are some fun things you can do with extra granola, but for me it's great with milk for a quick and healthy breakfast.

Servings: Makes about 10 cups | Prep Time: 10 minutes | Total Time: 45 minutes

6 cups rolled oats

1 cup slivered almonds

½ cup roasted sunflower seeds

¼ cup toasted sesame seeds

1 teaspoon cinnamon

½ teaspoon ground nutmeg

½ teaspoon kosher salt

⅔ cup honey

1 cup dried cranberries

1. Preheat oven to 325°F.

2. Mix oats, almond slivers, sunflower and sesame seeds, cinnamon, nutmeg, and salt together in a large bowl.

3. Once oat mixture is evenly mixed, drizzle in honey and stir well to combine.

4. Spread out granola mixture on two baking sheets lined with parchment paper.

5. Bake the granola for 20 to 25 minutes, stirring every 5 minutes to prevent granola from burning. It will most likely cook faster on the outer edges of the pan, so stir it well to redistribute the heat. If the granola is burning or cooking too quickly, turn your oven down to 300°F and continue stirring regularly.

6. Remove from oven and let cool for a few minutes, then stir in dried fruit.

7. Store granola in an airtight container at room temperature for up to 3 weeks.

A Note on Oil

Many granola recipes call for a small amount of a neutral oil, which helps the granola clump and also makes it crispier. I've never been a huge fan of this addition, but you can definitely add 2 to 3 tablespoons of a neutral oil like safflower or vegetable oil to the basic granola recipe or any of the variations. Stir the oil in after the dry ingredients are mixed and proceed with the recipe as normal. The resulting granola will have larger clumps.

Five Granola Variations

Start with the basic granola recipe, including the cooking time and temperature, and then use the table below for substitutions. Be sure to stir every 5 minutes during cooking to prevent burning.

VARIATION	INGREDIENTS	NOTES
Double Ginger Spice	Substitute 1 cup chopped hazelnuts for sunflower and sesame seeds Add 2 teaspoons ground ginger Add ¼ cup crystallized chopped ginger (Crystallized ginger is much cheaper if you buy it in the bulk section of your store rather than in the spice section.)	Add chopped hazelnuts to the oats with ground ginger and other ingredients. Stir together, add honey, and bake as normal. After baking, add dried cranberries and crystallized ginger.
Date Dream	Substitute 1 cup chopped walnuts for sunflower and sesame seeds Add 2 teaspoons vanilla extract Substitute 1 cup chopped dates for dried cranberries	Add chopped walnuts to the oat mixture and vanilla with the honey. Bake as normal. Stir in chopped dates while the granola cools.
Coconut Hazelnut	Substitute 1½ cups chopped hazelnuts for almonds and sesame seeds Add 1½ cups unsweetened shredded coconut Add 2 teaspoons vanilla extract	Bake as normal with all ingredients stirred together. Watch closely as the coconut will easily burn. Stir regularly. Remove when coconut is lightly toasted, about 20 minutes.
Pistachio Cherry	Substitute 1 cup chopped pistachios for the original almonds and sesame seeds Add 1 teaspoon vanilla extract Substitute dried cherries for cranberries	Bake normally with pistachios in the mix. Add cherries after baking.
Espresso	Nuts are optional for this version. Subtract seeds. Add 3 tablespoons instant espresso mixed with ⅓ cup water Add 1 teaspoon vanilla extract Add ⅓ cup unsalted butter Subtract dried cranberries Add 1 cup chocolate chips (optional)	Combine instant espresso mixed with water, vanilla, butter, spices, salt, and honey in a small saucepan. Heat on low until butter is melted and honey is dissolved. Pour hot mixture over oats and toss to combine. Mixture will be slightly wet. Bake as normal, but you will probably need to add 5 to 10 minutes to the baking time. Add chocolate chips if you're using them. Personally, I like it without chocolate.

Nut Butter Granola Bars

Any granola that's good will also be good in bar form, so feel free to use any of the variations or just the basic granola recipe for these bars. Once you have your granola cooked up, these are really simple to make and are a tasty snack for the road.

Servings: 10–12 bars (8 x 8-inch baking dish) | Prep Time: 15 minutes | Total Time: 15 minutes plus chilling time

½ **cup honey**

½ **cup nut butter (I prefer peanut butter)**

⅓ **cup brown sugar**

¼ **cup sunflower oil or any neutral oil**

4 **cups prepared granola**

1. Mix honey, nut butter, brown sugar, and oil in a medium saucepan over medium heat. Stir until it begins to bubble and all the ingredients are melted together.

2. Pour the hot syrup over the granola in a large bowl. Stir well.

3. Pack the mixture into an 8 x 8-inch baking dish. Press down on it to compress the oats.

4. Refrigerate for at least 2 hours.

5. Slice into ten to twelve even bars and store in an airtight bag; they will keep fine for a few weeks.

Three Berry Parfait

This is a classic breakfast item, and with good reason. It combines three terrific breakfast foods: granola, yogurt, and fruit. The key to parfait success is all about the ratio. Don't screw with the ratio.

If you can't find good fresh berries, frozen are okay. You can also make these guys the night before and store them in the fridge so breakfast is ready and waiting when you wake up.

Servings: 2 large parfaits | Prep Time: 15 minutes | Total Time: 15 minutes

1⅓ cups yogurt

1⅓ cups granola

1⅓ cups fresh or frozen berries (I like blueberries, blackberries, and strawberries)

2 tablespoons honey

1. If you are using frozen berries, thaw them on low power in the microwave until they are just thawed. You don't want them warm at all. Once they are thawed, drain them on a few paper towels so some of the liquid can be removed.

2. Add ⅓ cup yogurt to each of two tall, slender glasses.

3. Top with ⅓ cup granola in each glass. Drizzle the granola with a small amount of honey.

4. Top with ⅓ cup berries.

5. Repeat the layers using the same amounts. Sprinkle a bit of extra granola on top if you wish.

6. Serve immediately, or make the night before and store in the fridge.

Baked Apples

I'm sure you've heard of breakfast for dinner. Well, this is breakfast for dessert. While I originally thought these would be ideal for breakfast (and they are), I actually prefer them as a slightly healthy dessert option. Each serving has a whole apple and granola, so compared to other dessert options, it's not so bad.

Servings: 2 apples | Prep Time: 10 minutes | Total Time: 45 minutes

1. Preheat oven to 350°F.

2. Mix granola, brown sugar, cinnamon, nutmeg, and salt in a small bowl.

3. Core apples using an apple corer or paring knife. Clean out the inside well so you have a nice clean cavity for your granola stuffing.

4. Spoon ¼ cup granola mixture into each apple and top with a square of butter.

5. Bake apples for about 30 minutes. They should be slightly soft, but not mushy at all. You should be able to cut them with a butter knife.

6. Let apples cool for a minute and then serve immediately. Use a spatula when removing from the baking dish, or the filling will fall out the bottom of the apple.

½ cup granola

2 tablespoons brown sugar

Pinch of cinnamon

Pinch of ground nutmeg

Pinch of salt

2 large baking apples (I like Macintosh or Honey Crisp)

1 tablespoon unsalted butter

Granola Muffins

This is one of those recipes that will look like a mistake when you toss all the ingredients in the bowl. It doesn't have much flour and has a lot of granola. Just go with it! The resulting muffins are dense and flavorful and really delicious with a small pat of butter and a cup of coffee.

Servings: 12 muffins | Prep Time: 10 minutes | Total Time: 45 minutes

1. Preheat oven to 375°F.

2. Mix together granola, flour, brown sugar, baking powder, cinnamon, and salt in a medium bowl.

3. In a separate smaller bowl, whisk together buttermilk, melted butter, yogurt, egg, and vanilla until well combined.

4. Stir wet ingredients into dry ingredients until just combined. Try not to overmix the batter.

5. Spoon batter into a lightly greased muffin tin. Fill the tins almost to the top. You should get about twelve muffins.

6. Bake muffins for 18 to 20 minutes. Test a muffin to make sure it is cooked in the center. Let muffins cool for a few minutes before eating. They are best eaten right away, warm, with a little butter.

2 cups granola

1 cup all-purpose flour

⅓ cup brown sugar

2 teaspoons baking powder

½ teaspoon cinnamon

¼ teaspoon table salt

¾ cup buttermilk (or milk)

¼ cup unsalted butter, melted and cooled

¼ cup yogurt

1 large egg

1 teaspoon vanilla extract

High-altitude changes: Reduce baking powder to 1¾ teaspoons. Raise oven temperature to 400°F. Reduce baking time by 1 to 2 minutes.

Spinach Salad with Granola Topper

If you find yourself with an annoyingly small amount of granola left over, this is a perfect recipe for it. It's a quick and simple three-ingredient salad with a homemade dressing that brings all the ingredients together. You can use almost any granola for this recipe, but I would avoid the granola recipes with chocolate.

Servings: 2 side salads | Prep Time: 5 minutes | Total Time: 5 minutes

¼ cup Greek yogurt

1 tablespoon fresh lemon juice

1 tablespoon buttermilk (or milk)

1 teaspoon honey

Pinch of salt

2 cups baby spinach

Small handful of dried cranberries

½ cup granola

1. Whisk together the yogurt with the lemon juice, buttermilk, honey, and a pinch of salt. If you don't have buttermilk, you can substitute normal milk, but buttermilk works best.

2. Divide spinach between two bowls and sprinkle with a few dried cranberries.

3. Drizzle salad dressing over greens and top salads with granola of your choice.

Baked Sweet Potatoes

"You want me to eat granola for dinner," said my very patient, very loving wife.

"Absolutely," I replied, a bit hesitantly. She took a first bite and I crossed my fingers under the table.

"Oh, yeah. This'll work," she said.

It most certainly does work. In fact, a large one of these plus a side salad makes for a really delicious dinner. It wouldn't be a bad brunch item either!

Servings: 4 potatoes | Prep Time: 10 minutes | Total Time: 1 hour

1. Take a fork and poke a few holes in each potato. Bake on a sheet pan at 350°F for about an hour. When they are fork tender, they are done. In a pinch you can also wrap them in paper towels and microwave them on high for 8 to 10 minutes until tender.

2. Remove potatoes from oven (or microwave) and slice them open down the center. Use a fork to lightly mash the flesh.

3. Top each potato with about ¼ cup granola, a pinch of salt, a drizzle of maple syrup, and some chopped chives. Serve immediately!

4 large sweet potatoes

1 cup granola

Pinch of salt

3–4 tablespoons maple syrup

Chopped chives

Granola Apple Pie

I'm not one to lie about my cooking abilities, and so I'll be first to admit that pies are not my strongest skill. Pie perfection is a pretty tough thing to achieve. I always tell people that the only way to learn to make a perfect pie is to make a thousand pies. At the same time, the way to make a great pie is just to make a pie. Give it a go and you'll probably have a good result. It's pretty hard to go wrong really.

Sure, there are people who will tell you that you have to make your crust from scratch or that you have to use butter or lard for said crust (I'm in the butter camp), but in reality it doesn't matter. Granted, one version might be slightly more delicious than another, but you'll still wind up with a pie and that makes you a winner.

There's no doubt that granola and baked apples were made to be together, so topping an apple pie with a crunchy, thick granola layer just makes sense.

Servings: 8–12 slices (9-inch pie pan) | Prep Time: 30 minutes | Total Time: 3 hours

Basic Butter Pie Crust

½ teaspoon table salt

1½ cups all-purpose flour

½ cup (1 stick) unsalted butter, cold

2 tablespoons vodka (optional)

3–5 tablespoons ice cold water

Filling

3 pounds (6–7 large) Granny Smith apples

⅓ cup sugar

¼ cup brown sugar

2 tablespoons all-purpose flour

2 teaspoons cinnamon

1 tablespoon lemon juice

Pinch of salt

1. **To make pie crust:** Mix salt and flour in a medium bowl. Cube butter into chunks. Use your fingers or a fork to mash the butter into the flour and salt. The butter should resemble pea-size balls in the flour.

2. Add vodka and ice water by the tablespoon to the flour mixture. If you don't want to use vodka, increase the ice water until the dough just comes together. Try not to use too much water or the dough will become tough later.

3. Once the dough is in rough pieces, turn it out onto a dry, clean surface. Press it together until it forms a ball. Wrap it in plastic and chill for at least an hour in the fridge to firm up.

4. **For filling:** Meanwhile, peel and core apples and slice them into thin wedges. Stir with other filling ingredients (sugars, flour, cinnamon, lemon juice, and salt) and put in a colander over the sink so the filling can drain. Let sit for 30 minutes.

5. **For topping:** Stir together granola, sugars, cinnamon, and salt until it is well mixed. Stir in melted butter and let sit until needed.

6. When you're ready to make the pie, preheat oven to 375°F.

7. Roll out your pie crust on a lightly floured surface. Work slowly and carefully, and don't worry if the crust cracks a bit. Carefully fold and pick up the crust and place it in a 9-inch pie pan. If you have any cracks or holes in the crust, patch them with extra crust that you probably have from the rolling process.

8. Crimp the edge of the crust around the edge of the pie pan. I just pinch the dough between my two index fingers as I work around to form a basic edge.

9. Fill pie with the drained apple filling. Completely cover the apples with the granola topping.

10. Bake pie in the center of the oven until the granola topping is a dark brown color and the apples are cooked through, about 80 to 90 minutes. Check the pie after an hour, and if the crust is browning too much, then cover the edges with foil and return to the oven.

11. Remove the pie and let it cool for at least 20 minutes before serving.

Topping

1½ cups granola

⅓ cup sugar

⅓ cup brown sugar

½ teaspoon cinnamon

½ teaspoon kosher salt

6 tablespoons unsalted butter, melted

Note: Adding vodka to pie crust dough is a nice trick that makes it easier to roll out. The vodka evaporates quickly in the oven, leaving you with a flaky crust.

Granola Tiramisu

Italians: Look away! This is undoubtedly sacrilege to the traditional Italian dessert, but it's delicious sacrilege. The thing about traditional tiramisu is that you have to find or make ladyfinger cakes, which are tricky to make and sometimes impossible to find, depending on where you live. But all you really need to make a good tiramisu is something that soaks up the delicious coffee/liquor mixture, and granola does the trick!

You can use any granola variation or a mixture for this recipe. My personal favorite is the cherry and pistachio variation. If you use the espresso granola variation, reduce the instant espresso in the recipe.

Servings: 8 (8 x 8-inch pan) | Prep Time: 20 minutes | Total Time: 30 minutes plus chilling time

1. Stir together instant espresso, milk, and brandy or bourbon. Pour over granola and let sit for 5 minutes so the granola soaks up the liquid mixture. Stir a few times to make sure the liquid is getting distributed evenly over the oats.

2. In the bowl of a stand mixer or just a mixing bowl, combine cream and mascarpone and beat on medium-high until it forms stiff peaks, about 4 minutes.

3. Add in vanilla, then slowly add in powdered sugar in three or four batches. Mix thoroughly.

4. Spread half the granola mixture in an 8 x 8-inch baking dish. Top with half the mascarpone mixture. Dust generously with cocoa powder and cinnamon.

5. Repeat layers with the rest of the granola and the last of the mascarpone cheese mixture. Again, dust heavily with cinnamon and cocoa powder.

6. Let chill in the fridge for at least 3 to 4 hours before serving.

Note: If you don't want to use instant espresso, you can also use 1 cup of very strong coffee in place of the milk and espresso.

3 tablespoons instant espresso (1½ if you are using espresso granola)

1 cup milk

⅓ cup brandy or bourbon

4 cups granola (any of the variations would be good)

1 cup heavy cream

1 pound mascarpone cheese

1 teaspoon vanilla extract

1 cup powdered sugar

Cinnamon, for dusting

Cocoa powder, for dusting

CHAPTER 12

RICE

I challenge you to make the exact amount of rice you need for a meal. I think it's impossible. You either fall short or have leftovers. It's some unwritten physical rule of the kitchen that the rice in the pot will expand or contract to make sure you never have the perfect amount you need.

To solve this problem, I just cook a bunch of it, because more is better than not enough. This is especially true when dealing with a food like rice that keeps well and can be used in dozens of different ways. It's one of the most consumed foods on the planet for a reason.

The problem with rice is actually cooking it. Many people think it's a pain in the butt. That's why there's a whole market of contraptions and gadgets that revolve around cooking rice. Don't worry. You don't need any of that fancy equipment to properly cook rice. After all, I can guarantee you that the nice Andean lady who cooks perfect rice and sells it out of a cart in Peru doesn't have a Rice Maker MAX 5000. She has a pot, rice, and water. That's all she needs, and it's all you need.

The method I describe in this chapter for cooking rice, which is essentially boiling and steaming it, is one of my favorite cooking techniques in this entire book. If you master it (it isn't hard), then you can cook almost any rice and never be left with a pot of mush or a burned, blackened pot. And you can give your Rice Maker MAX 5000 to one of your rice-loving friends. Actually, scratch that. Just give them a copy of this book with this chapter earmarked.

The Perfect Rice Method

Cooking rice according to the directions on packaging is one of the most frustrating things in the kitchen. They always give you directions to measure out precise amounts of water and rice and cook it for a very specific amount of time.

When I used to try to follow these instructions, I always wound up in two boats. Boat A would result in a big pot of mush. Boat B would lead to burned rice stuck to a pan. It seemed almost impossible to get right.

That method is just plain stupid.

The truth is you can cook rice just like you cook pasta. You don't need specific measurements or exact timing. And you definitely don't need a fancy piece of equipment.

The method below works with almost any kind of rice: short grain to long grain, white rice or brown rice. The only kind of rice it won't work with is any sort of pre-cooked, dried rice. So it won't work with instant rice.

Servings: Depends on the rice used; read package information | Prep Time: Depends on the rice used; read package information

1 pound rice (you can cook less, but it makes sense to cook a large batch)

Water

Pinch of salt (optional)

1. Add rice to a large pot. Fill pot with cold water and swirl rice in the water to rinse it well. Carefully pour out most of the cold water (it's okay if you lose some rice) and re-rinse the rice. Keep rinsing until the water is mostly clear. This will probably take three or four rinses, depending on the rice you are using.

2. Once your rice is clean, fill the pot with hot water. There should be at least a few inches of water above the rice line. I always use at least a 4-quart pot and add water until it covers the rice by 4 to 5 inches. Add a pinch of salt (if you're using it). Stir the rice to separate the grains in the water, cover, and place over high heat.

3. Once the water starts to simmer, remove lid or it will probably boil over. Turn down heat to medium-high.

4. As the rice boils, spoon out a few grains every 5 minutes or so and taste it. Keep cooking until the rice is almost cooked through. It should have a very tiny bite to it. In pasta terms it would be al dente. If ever the water looks murky or starts to get thick, add more water to keep the grains moving.

5. As soon as the rice is almost cooked to the right texture (see below for some guidelines), drain the rice using a wire mesh colander that the rice can't fit through. If you are using quicker-cooking rice like short-grained white rice, be sure to drain off as much water as possible or you'll run the risk of overcooking the rice later.

6. Once you've drained off most of the water, pour the rice back into the hot pan immediately. Return the pan to the stove, cover, and cook on low heat for 30 seconds just to reheat the pan.

7. Turn off heat and let the rice steam, covered, for 8 minutes.

8. Uncover rice and fluff well with a fork to separate grains. Serve immediately or cool and store for later.

A Note on Cooking Time

Obviously, different rice varieties will require different cooking times using this boiling method. But the only step that changes in the preparation method is the amount of time you allow the rice to boil. I hesitate to give specific times for cooking different rice grains because it depends on a lot of variables like pot size and amount of rice you are cooking. You should just get into the habit of tasting it every few minutes until you get a general cooking time down for the variety of rice you cook most.

That said, I'll try to give some guidelines. Most white rice varieties will take 5 to 12 minutes of boiling to reach the right texture. Short grain white rice is the fastest and only needs to boil for few minutes. Long grain white rice or similar varieties like jasmine rice takes longer and will usually need to boil for around 10 to 12 minutes.

Brown rice and other heartier rice varieties like wild rice are different beasts entirely. They will take at least 15 to 20 minutes and possibly longer. Don't even bother tasting these varieties until they've boiled for at least 10 minutes.

Again, regardless of the variety, instant rice will not work with this method. It's already cooked and dehydrated, so cooking it again using this boiling method will turn it to mush.

Storing the Rice

Unless you run a Chinese food restaurant in your spare time, you probably won't be able to finish a pound of rice in one sitting. The important thing to remember about storing rice is to always make sure it cools off first. You should never store rice hot, as it will collect condensation and become soggy.

You can keep cooked rice in the fridge for up to a week without any problems. Occasionally rice will get dry when it's stored. If that happens to your rice, you can microwave it with a few tablespoons of water or a knob of butter and it will come back to life.

If you want to store your rice for the long term, you can wrap up individual portions of rice (3/4 cup is my portion size) in plastic wrap. Add the rice to the center of a square of plastic and then twist the ends to form an airtight pouch. Freeze these individual servings in a freezer-safe bag and they will keep for months.

When you need a few portions of rice, unwrap and remove them from the plastic wrap. Microwave rice with about a tablespoon of water per 3/4 cup rice on high in 30-second bursts until the rice is hot and ready to serve.

Breakfast Congee

This is one of my favorite things to make with leftover rice from Chinese take-out food. The recipe works best with starchy short or medium grain white rice, so leftover take-out rice is perfect. I have no idea why this sort of breakfast hasn't really caught on in America. It's delicious, almost like savory oatmeal, and is a surefire cure for any hangover you can throw at it.

Servings: 2 | Prep Time: 10 minutes | Total Time: 40 minutes

3 cups water

1 cup chicken stock

1½ cups cooked white rice

Salt and pepper

1 teaspoon neutral oil (canola or vegetable oil)

4 ounces ham slices

2 eggs, soft-boiled or fried

Fresh cilantro, garnish

Chopped scallions, garnish

Sriracha chili sauce

1. To start the congee, add the water, stock, and cooked rice to a medium pot with a pinch of salt. Bring the mixture to a boil over medium heat and then reduce the heat to medium-low.

2. Simmer the rice, uncovered, for 30 minutes. Stir it occasionally. You can prep your other ingredients while the congee cooks. The rice should thicken and almost dissolve in the liquid as it cooks. The final congee should be very thick, almost like runny oatmeal.

3. While the rice cooks, add a drizzle of oil to a skillet over medium heat and sear a few pieces of ham for a few minutes per side.

4. **To soft-boil your eggs:** Bring about ½ inch of water to a simmer in a heavy pot with a lid over high heat. Once simmering, take your large or extra large eggs straight from the fridge and gently place them in the simmering water. The water won't cover the eggs. That's okay.

5. Cover the pot with a lid and set a timer for exactly 6 minutes 30 seconds. It's very important that the pot is over high heat because the goal is to return the water to a simmer as soon as possible.

6. When they have steamed for that exact amount of time, immediately move the pot to the sink and rinse the eggs with very cold water for 30 seconds.

7. Peel the eggs carefully, starting at the wide end of the egg. Slightly older eggs will be easier to peel. If peeling eggs is the bane of your existence, you can also just fry the eggs in a bit of butter or oil.

8. Once the congee is thick, season it well with salt and pepper. Ladle the congee into two bowls and top each bowl with some of the ham, an egg, fresh cilantro, scallions, and a drizzle of chili sauce.

Ginger Pineapple Fried Rice

The key to making a good fried rice dish, like many dishes, is to make sure you have all your chopping and prep done before you even heat the pan. The whole meal cooks in almost no time, and if you turn your back on your hot skillet or wok, the dish will burn.

So take your time chopping and mincing and then focus on cooking the ingredients over very high heat as quickly as possible. You'll be well rewarded.

Servings: 4 | Prep Time: 30 minutes | Total Time: 45 minutes

1. For this fried rice, be sure to take your time dicing the vegetables and pineapple. Make sure to mince the garlic, ginger, and shallot finely. For the pineapple, cut off the ends, then stand it on its end and cut the rind off around the edges. Next, cut it in quarters and remove the light-yellow core, which is a bit tough to chew. Then dice the flesh into ½-inch cubes.

2. Whisk together the soy sauce, fish sauce, rice wine vinegar, and red pepper flakes in a small bowl.

3. Whisk eggs well in another small bowl.

4. In a large wok or skillet, add oil over high heat. Once hot, add the pineapple and cook until pineapple starts to caramelize slightly, about 5 minutes.

5. Add ginger, shallot, and garlic to the pan and cook for another 1 to 2 minutes, stirring constantly.

6. Add sauce to the pan followed by cooked rice. Toss everything together and cook for 30 seconds.

7. Make a well in the center of the pan and pour eggs in the center. Let sit for 30 seconds and then stir everything together.

8. Finally, add peas and toss to heat through and combine flavors.

9. Garnish with red pepper flakes and fresh cilantro. Serve immediately with extra soy sauce.

4 cloves garlic, minced

¼ cup minced fresh ginger

⅓ cup minced shallot

1½ cups diced fresh pineapple

2 tablespoons soy sauce

1 tablespoon fish sauce

1 tablespoon rice wine vinegar

½–1 teaspoon red pepper flakes

4 large eggs

¼ cup vegetable oil

4–5 cups cooked rice (long grain white rice is best)

1 cup frozen peas, thawed

Fresh cilantro, garnish

Note: You can use canned pineapple in a pinch. Just drain it well so there isn't a lot of liquid on the pineapple. Fresh is definitely best though.

Rice-Stuffed Red Peppers

You could use any pepper for this dish obviously, but I think red peppers have the best flavor when cooked. Most people will cut the stem off the top of the peppers to stuff them, but then it's hard to get them to stay upright when baking. Instead, slice off the side of each pepper and let them lie naturally on their sides.

Servings: 6 (5 if you have super-large red peppers) | Prep Time: 20 minutes | Total Time: 1 hour

6 red peppers

2 tablespoons olive oil

1 cup diced white onion

2 cloves garlic, minced

1 Serrano pepper, minced

2 teaspoons paprika

1 (28-ounce) can diced tomatoes

2 cups cooked rice

Salt and pepper

1 cup shredded Pepper Jack cheese

½ cup grated Parmesan cheese, garnish

Fresh parsley, garnish

1. Preheat oven to 350°F.

2. Sit red peppers upright and slice off one side. Clean out each pepper, removing the guts and seeds. Save the pepper slices for a salad!

3. In a medium pot, add olive oil over medium heat. Once hot, add the onions, garlic, and Serrano pepper and cook until the veggies are soft, about 5 minutes.

4. Add paprika and cook for a minute. Then add diced tomatoes and cook the mixture for 10 to 15 minutes, mashing the tomatoes to break them down as it cooks.

5. Once the tomato sauce thickens slightly, stir in cooked rice and remove the pot from the heat. Be careful not to cook the sauce once you add the cooked rice or the rice will turn to mush.

6. Season the mixture with salt and pepper and stir in shredded cheese, which should melt from the heat of the sauce. Don't worry if the mixture looks slightly runny at this point. It will firm up more as it bakes in the peppers.

7. Once the filling has cooled for a minute or two, spoon some into each pepper, filling each pepper to the top.

8. Bake peppers on an ungreased baking sheet until the peppers are cooked, but still a bit firm, 30 to 35 minutes.

9. Remove peppers from oven, garnish with grated Parmesan cheese and fresh parsley, and serve immediately.

Minted Rice Salad

This is a nice, light salad that pairs well with a ton of dishes. If you happen to be a lamb fan, try it with some seared lamb chops. Personally, I love this salad as a lunch salad. It's surprisingly filling. And yes, you better believe I squirt a good amount of Sriracha on top if I'm eating it for lunch.

Servings: 4 as a side or starter | Prep Time: 15 minutes | Total Time: 15 minutes

Dressing:

¼ cup minced shallot

1 clove garlic, minced

3 tablespoons extra-virgin olive oil

1 tablespoon honey

1 tablespoon soy sauce

1 tablespoon rice wine vinegar

1 tablespoon lemon juice

1 teaspoon toasted sesame oil

Pinch of black pepper

4 cups cooked rice

1 cup diced cucumbers

1 cup frozen edamame or peas, thawed

1 cup chopped radish (about 6 radishes)

3 tablespoons minced fresh mint

1. **For dressing:** Whisk together the dressing ingredients in a small bowl.

2. Stir together rice with vegetables and mint in a large bowl. If your rice is very dry and crispy, I recommend microwaving it on high for 30 seconds with 2 tablespoons water to soften it.

3. Pour dressing over salad and stir well.

4. Serve immediately or store in the fridge. The salad will keep fine for a few days.

Chicken and Rice Soup

I wrote this recipe as a stand-alone recipe, but it pairs perfectly with the Roast Chicken chapter in this book. If you happen to have some shredded chicken and chicken stock left over from that chapter, this is a must-make, especially on a cold day. It's really flavorful, healthy, and warming.

Of course, you don't need to have those things to make the recipe. It's plenty good with store-bought stock and freshly cooked chicken.

Servings: 4–6 | Prep Time: 15 minutes |
Total Time: 40 minutes

1. Bring a medium pot of water to a simmer over medium-high heat and add chicken. Reduce heat to medium, cover the pot, and poach until chicken is cooked through, about 15 minutes. Drain, let chicken cool briefly, and shred chicken meat. Alternatively, you can use shredded chicken from the Roast Chicken chapter.

2. In a large pot, add olive oil over medium heat. Stir in onions, celery, carrots, and garlic and season with a pinch of salt. Cook until onions turn translucent, about 5 minutes. Be careful not to burn garlic.

3. Add shredded chicken, chicken stock, and optional red pepper flakes and bring to a simmer. Simmer for 5 to 10 minutes so flavors can combine.

4. Add lemon juice and cooked rice and stir together. Once you add rice, don't simmer for too long or the rice will turn mushy.

5. Season soup with salt and pepper, garnish with freshly chopped parsley, and serve immediately with lots of crusty bread or crackers!

1 pound chicken breasts, poached and shredded

1 tablespoon olive oil

1 cup diced white onion (about 1 medium onion)

2 stalks celery, minced

1 medium carrot, sliced into half rounds

1 clove garlic, minced

Salt and pepper

1 quart chicken stock

¼ teaspoon red pepper flakes (optional)

1 small lemon, juice only

2 cups cooked rice

Freshly chopped parsley, garnish

Tomato Basil Arancini

Arancini, stuffed and fried rice balls, are traditionally made with leftover risotto, but there's no rule I've read that says you have to make them with risotto. I make them with all kinds of leftover rice. The key is to make sure that your rice is sticky enough to hold together, which might require adding a bit of extra liquid to it.

Servings: 12–14 large arancini | Prep Time: 30 minutes | Total Time: 45 minutes

3 cups cooked rice (medium grain works well)

½ cup sun-dried tomatoes from oil (about a 7-ounce jar)

1 cup lightly packed minced fresh basil

1 teaspoon red pepper flakes

½ teaspoon kosher salt

1 tablespoon oil from sun-dried tomatoes

3–4 ounces manchego or other semi-hard cheese

1 cup all-purpose flour

1 teaspoon each salt and pepper

3 large eggs, whisked

1½ cups bread crumbs

2 quarts vegetable or canola oil for frying

Note: If your rice doesn't stick together and is still too dry, add another tablespoon or two of the oil from the sun-dried tomatoes plus 1 tablespoon all-purpose flour, which should make it sticky.

1. If your rice is very dry out of the fridge and has a crunchy texture, microwave it for 30 seconds with two tablespoons of water to loosen it up and make it easier to shape.

2. Chop sun-dried tomatoes very finely and stir into cooked rice. Add minced basil, red pepper flakes, salt, and 1 tablespoon oil from the sun-dried tomato jar.

3. Cube cheese into ¼-inch cubes. You need one cube for each rice ball, so judge accordingly.

4. Scoop out ¼ cup of the rice mixture into your hand and stick a cube of cheese right in the center of the rice. Use your hands to shape the rice around the cube of cheese and pack it into a tight ball. Set the finished ball on a baking sheet and repeat until the rice mixture is gone.

5. In three bowls, mix the flour plus a big pinch of salt and pepper in one bowl, the eggs in a second bowl, and the bread crumbs in the third.

6. Working with one ball at a time, roll the ball in the flour, then in the egg mixture, then in the bread crumbs. Use your hands to make sure the bread crumbs are packed on nicely and return the ball to the baking sheet. Repeat with all the rice balls.

7. Heat the oil to 350°F in a large, sturdy pot. Please, use a deep-fry thermometer to make sure you don't overheat the oil.

8. Working in two or three batches, depending on the size of your pot, fry the rice balls for 4 to 5 minutes until they are golden brown.

9. Remove arancini to a plate lined with paper towels to drain for a few minutes and then serve immediately.

10. You can keep cooked arancini warm in a 250°F oven while you fry the other batches.

Tex-Mex Variation

If you want to try something different, I sometimes make these arancini with more of a Tex-Mex spin on them.

2 tablespoons olive oil

½ small red onion, minced

3 cups cooked rice (medium grain works well)

1 (15-ounce) can diced tomatoes

1 (4-ounce) can diced green chiles

½ teaspoon kosher salt

1 teaspoon red pepper flakes

1 teaspoon ground cumin

1 avocado, diced

2 tablespoons cilantro (optional)

3–4 ounces Pepper Jack cheese

1 cup all-purpose flour

1 teaspoon kosher salt

1 teaspoon black pepper

3 large eggs, whisked

1½ cups bread crumbs

2 quarts vegetable or canola oil for frying

1. In a medium pan over medium heat, add oil followed by red onion. Cook until the onion is soft, about 4 minutes.

2. Add rice, tomatoes, and chiles to the pot and cook for a few minutes. Add salt, red pepper flakes, and cumin.

3. Remove from heat and let cool until you can work with the rice mixture. If the mixture is very wet, press down on the rice with a few paper towels to draw out some of the liquid. Try forming a ball out of the rice to make sure it is sticky, but not too wet.

4. Add in avocado and cilantro (if you're using it) once the rice is relatively cool.

5. Continue with the arancini recipe using Pepper Jack cheese in place of manchego cheese.

Arroz Mixto

I debated long and hard about whether or not to include this recipe in this book, even though it's one of my favorite things to do with leftover rice. I thought about not including it because it doesn't look like a sexy recipe. But then I slapped some sense into myself and remembered that this book isn't about foo-foo dishes. It's about delicious dishes.

This is a traditional South American plate. You'll find some riff on it in almost every market in South America. It's sometimes served with fried potatoes as well, but I think they are kind of overkill unless you happen to live in the high Andes.

Servings: 2 | Prep Time: 10 minutes | Total Time: 20 minutes

1. Add cooked rice to a microwave-safe bowl with butter and a pinch of salt and pepper. Microwave on high for 90 seconds to reheat rice.

2. In a medium skillet, cook sausages with a drizzle of oil over medium heat until they are nicely browned on all sides and cooked through. For this meal, I actually like starting with fully cooked chicken sausages, but you could use any sausage.

3. Once the sausage is done cooking (about 10 to 15 minutes), remove it from the pan and add another drizzle of oil. Crack in two eggs and fry them for about 90 seconds. Then flip and fry for another 15 seconds so they are soft-cooked.

4. Divide rice between two plates. Top rice with chopped-up sausage, the fried egg, sliced avocado, a spoonful of salsa, cucumber slices, banana peppers, scallions, and cilantro.

5. Season the dish with crushed red pepper flakes, salt, and pepper and serve immediately.

2 cups cooked rice

1 tablespoon unsalted butter

Salt and pepper

2 sausages (I prefer chicken for my version)

1 tablespoon vegetable oil

2 large eggs

1 avocado, sliced

¼ cup spicy salsa

½ cup sliced cucumber

Pickled banana peppers

Chopped scallions

Fresh cilantro

Red pepper flakes

Broccoli Cheddar Casserole

This recipe reminds me a lot of a casserole that I used to eat as a child. I believe that the dish I had as a child was made with broccoli soup, so this version is a bit different and has nice big pieces of broccoli throughout the casserole. It's super cheesy and filling though. If you want to get your kids to eat their broccoli, this is one way to do it.

Servings: 4–6 | Prep Time: 30 minutes | Total Time: 1 hour

9–10 ounces (about 3 cups) chopped broccoli florets

1 cup heavy cream

½ cup milk

1 cup chicken stock

3 tablespoons olive oil

½ medium onion, diced

3 cloves garlic, minced

¼ teaspoon cayenne pepper (optional)

½ teaspoon red pepper flakes

Salt and pepper

3 tablespoons flour

8 ounces (about 2 packed cups) grated cheddar cheese

3 cups cooked rice

⅓ cup slivered almonds

1. Preheat oven to 400°F.

2. Butter or lightly grease a large 2½-quart baking dish. (If you use a standard 8 x 8-inch baking dish, you might have some casserole left over, as an 8 x 8-inch dish will hold roughly 2 quarts. It will work even if you don't have the exact size I used.)

3. In a medium pot, bring water to a simmer and salt it with about a tablespoon of kosher salt. Once simmering, add broccoli florets and cook for 60 seconds. Drain florets and rinse with cold water to stop cooking. They should be slightly crunchy still. Set broccoli florets aside for later. I like my broccoli to be in big chunks, but you can also dice into smaller bites.

Note: You can use frozen broccoli. Just thaw it in the microwave and skip this step.

4. In a medium pot, combine cream, milk, and stock over medium-low heat and warm the mixture until it's steaming, but not simmering. Keep it warm over low heat until needed.

5. In a second, larger pot, add oil over medium heat followed by diced onion and garlic. Cook until soft, about 4 minutes. Add cayenne (if you're using it), red pepper flakes, and a pinch of salt and pepper to the pot. Stir to combine.

6. Add flour to the pot and use a whisk to stir the flour into the oil, forming a roux. Cook the roux until it is a light tan color, about 4 to 5 minutes.

7. Slowly ladle in the warm cream mixture. Whisk constantly as you add the hot liquid to the roux base. It should thicken immediately. Continue to add liquid to the pot until it is all combined. Whisk well and bring to a slight simmer. The mixture should be the consistency of thin gravy. If it is very thin, simmer for a minute or two to thicken it.

8. Add grated cheese and stir until cheese is melted.

9. Stir in broccoli and rice. Taste the mixture and season with salt and pepper.

10. Add casserole mixture to prepared baking dish. Bake for 15 minutes.

11. Add slivered almonds to the top of the dish and bake for another 15 minutes.

12. Remove casserole and let cool for a few minutes before serving.

Coconut Rice Pudding

Rice can be surprisingly delicious in dessert. I especially like it because I don't like super-sweet desserts. I like my desserts to have good flavors and creamy textures, but I'm rarely looking for something nutso sweet. While this pudding would be very sweet on its own, the rice actually cuts some of the sweetness and makes it work.

Servings: 6 | Prep Time: 30 minutes | Total Time: 45 minutes plus 4 hours chilling

1 cup shredded, unsweetened coconut flakes

2 large eggs

2 large egg yolks

1 cup sugar, divided

1 tablespoon cornstarch

1 tablespoon vanilla extract

1½ cups milk

1 cup coconut milk

½ teaspoon kosher salt

2 cups cooked rice

¼ cup heavy whipping cream

1. In a dry skillet, toast coconut over low heat until it's lightly browned, about 6 to 8 minutes, depending on your coconut and pan. Stir the coconut regularly to make sure it toasts evenly, and don't turn your back on this as it will burn. If you have large shreds of coconut, crush them into smaller bits with your hands after it cools.

2. In a medium bowl, whisk together the eggs, yolks, ½ cup sugar, cornstarch, and vanilla. Set aside.

3. In a medium-large pot, add milk and coconut milk with salt. Bring to almost a simmer over medium-low heat, stirring frequently to make sure the milk doesn't scald.

4. When milk is steaming and almost at a simmer, remove it from the heat and slowly pour half of it into the egg mixture, whisking constantly while you add it. Once half of the hot milk is whisked into egg mixture, pour that mixture back into the pot with the rest of the hot milk. Continue to whisk.

5. Continue to stir mixture over low heat. Let the mixture thicken over low heat for 3 to 4 minutes, stirring constantly. At this point it helps to switch from a whisk to a flat spatula while stirring.

6. Stir in rice and continue to simmer on low until the mixture is very thick, about 5 minutes.

7. Stir in heavy cream and three-quarters of the toasted coconut.

8. Remove from heat and pour pudding mixture into ramekins. You can either use small single-serving ramekins or just pour the mixture into a large 2½-quart dish. Either way, sprinkle the rest of the toasted coconut on top of the pudding.

9. Let the pudding cool at room temperature for 20 minutes, then cover with plastic wrap and transfer to the fridge to chill completely. Serve chilled.

CHAPTER 13

ROAST SALMON

Most cooks would tell you that you shouldn't strive to have a lot of leftover fish in your fridge. Most types of fish don't keep well, and it's true that fish tends to be at its best when it's fresh (or cured). But, if you cook fish regularly, you'll inevitably wind up with some extras. Maybe a dinner guest didn't show and you're left with a spare fillet, or one of your kids just flat-out refuses to try fish. It would be a serious shame to toss the extras because of neglect, so I felt it would be fun to show you a few ways that I use leftover fish on the few occasions that I have it.

I centered this entire chapter around salmon because it's a sturdy fish and will actually store better than many varieties. But that's not to say that other types of leftover fish can't be used in these recipes. I tried to craft the recipes to use flavors that pair well with a solid variety of seafood. Meatier fish varieties like tuna can be used in almost every recipe.

The other reason I like to use salmon for these recipes is because you can frequently find it in whole side fillets. A whole side of salmon can weigh a few pounds, so leftovers will be almost a given. It's actually my preferred way to cook salmon, because there's less chance of overcooking the fish. Also, the leftovers keep better for longer if they are kept in larger pieces.

When I started this chapter, I thought of it as an emergency plan, but after eating through the recipes a few times, I have no doubt that I'll make an extra salmon fillet every chance I get. Some of the recipes in this chapter will make you forget that you're eating three-day-old fish.

Herb-Roasted Salmon

This is about as simple and basic as salmon can get, but I don't see any reason to complicate seafood when it's fresh. Get a nice fresh side of salmon—I'm not a huge fan of farm-raised salmon—and treat it like doctors treat patients. First rule: Do no harm.

Servings: 6-8 | Prep Time: 5 minutes | Total Time: 30 minutes

2-3 pounds salmon, skin on

2 tablespoons olive oil

Pinch of kosher salt

1 lemon

1 tablespoon fresh dill

1. Preheat oven to 400°F.

2. Place your salmon skin-side down on a baking sheet. Run your fingers down the middle of the salmon and make sure there are no pin bones. Most butchers will remove them for you, but if you need to remove them yourself, the best tools to use are a clean pair of tweezers and a good dose of patience.

3. Once salmon is de-boned, drizzle the entire piece of fish with olive oil. Sprinkle lightly with kosher salt. Cut thin coins out of the lemon and dot the fish with the lemon pieces. Then sprinkle the surface of the fish with fresh dill.

4. Bake fish for 20 minutes. This should be just enough time to cook it through. If your salmon fillet is particularly thick, it might need another few minutes. When it is done, the salmon should flake apart easily.

5. Slice salmon into servings and serve immediately or store for later. If you want to remove skin before serving, slide a spatula between the salmon skin and flesh for easy removal.

Storing Salmon

Fish is notorious for not storing well, and it's true that it won't last as long as some of the other leftover bases in this book. That doesn't mean you won't occasionally find yourself with leftovers—and you shouldn't just toss them!

For best results, allow your salmon to cool completely to room temperature and then store it in airtight containers. Store the salmon in as large of pieces as possible and keep the skin on the salmon as well. This will help it keep longer. If stored correctly, it should last for 4 to 5 days.

I wouldn't bother freezing cooked salmon. It degrades pretty rapidly, and the thawed, cooked fish loses a lot of its texture.

Salmon Chips

Salmon is an expensive food. If you're buying whole fillets, a not insignificant portion of the fish will be skin. Most people just toss it. Not me! Skin actually makes for great snacks if prepared right. Think pork rinds except with seafood. These guys are super crispy and salty, and once people get over their preconceived weirdness of eating salmon skin, these chips will disappear from the table. You can use uncooked skin for this, but my preferred method is to cook the salmon, save the skin, and then make this recipe.

Servings: 4–6 | Prep Time: 10 minutes | Total Time: 30 minutes

Salmon skin

Neutral oil (vegetable, canola, or sunflower)

Kosher salt

1. Preheat oven to 350°F.

2. Grab two baking sheets that can easily nest inside each other. Cut two pieces of parchment paper to fit the baking sheets.

3. Make sure skin is relatively clean. It shouldn't have a lot of salmon on it, but some is okay.

4. Slice salmon skin into long ½-inch strips. Lay strips out on one baking sheet lined with parchment paper. Drizzle salmon skins very lightly with a neutral oil and sprinkle lightly with kosher salt.

5. Cover skins with another piece of parchment paper and then set the second baking sheet on top so it presses the skins flat.

6. Bake skins in between the two baking sheets for 20 to 25 minutes.

7. Remove from the oven and let cool slightly. Chips are great warm or at room temperature. They will continue to crisp up as they cool.

Salmon Scrambled Eggs

Smoked salmon is a common breakfast item, but the non-smoked fish works just as well in some dishes. The most important part of these eggs is to cook them slowly over relatively low heat so they remain nice and creamy and don't get too firm. Be gentle folding the salmon into the eggs at the end so it stays in nice chunks.

Servings: 2 | Prep Time: 5 minutes | Total Time: 15 minutes

1. In a medium pot, crack in eggs. Add butter and cream and put eggs over medium-low heat.

2. Stir eggs, breaking up the yolks in the pan, lightly scrambling them. Once the eggs are scrambled, let them sit over the heat until they begin to cook, then start stirring them constantly. You want them to cook slowly so as not to overcook them. If you do it right, it should take at least 10 minutes for the butter to melt and the eggs to turn soft and silky smooth. They shouldn't be dry and completely firm, but should have some curds forming.

3. When the eggs reach the desired consistency (cooked, but soft), turn down heat to very low and gently fold in flaked salmon. Season with salt and pepper. Let the eggs cook for just a minute more to warm the salmon through.

4. Garnish with fresh dill and serve immediately with toast pieces.

4 large eggs

1½ tablespoons unsalted butter

1 tablespoon heavy cream

4 ounces (⅔ cup) flaked cooked salmon

Salt and pepper

Fresh dill, garnish

Toast

Salmon Cakes

I would be a pretty bad food writer if I wrote an entire chapter about leftover fish and didn't include a recipe for fried cakes. Making little breaded cakes is probably the most popular way to use extra fish, and restaurants know that you can sell what are essentially leftovers at a premium. That's because they are damn good. I can eat these for breakfast, lunch, or as an appetizer.

Be gentle with the cakes as you shape and fry them. You want them to stay light and flaky. This is a recipe that is easily adaptable to other kinds of fish. Any flaky white fish would work just as well in these cakes.

Servings: 8 cakes | Prep Time: 15 minutes | Total Time: 40 minutes

1. Mince scallions (whites and greens), garlic, and dill very finely. Stir together with flaked salmon in a medium bowl. Try to keep the salmon in chunks. Don't stir it into a mush.

2. Stir in red pepper flakes, flour, Old Bay seasoning, and kosher salt.

3. Crack in an egg and mix it into the cake mixture. Then add bread crumbs and stir to combine.

4. Heat oil in a large skillet over medium-high heat. Measure out about ¼-cup cakes and press them into disks. They should be on the small side and just barely stick together.

5. Fry the cakes until they are lightly browned, about 4 to 5 minutes per side. Try to flip them only once, and don't fuss with them too much or they might break apart. If your pan isn't large enough to fit all the cakes, work in batches to make sure they brown nicely. (You can keep cooked cakes warm in a 200°F oven if you are working in batches.)

6. Remove cakes and let them drain on a few paper towels. Serve immediately with Greek yogurt and fresh dill.

2 scallions

1 clove garlic

1 tablespoon fresh dill

12 ounces (2 cups) flaked cooked salmon

½ teaspoon red pepper flakes

2 tablespoons all-purpose flour

½ teaspoon Old Bay seasoning

½ teaspoon kosher salt

1 large egg

½ cup panko bread crumbs

¼ cup vegetable oil, for frying

Greek yogurt, garnish

Fresh dill, garnish

Salmon Niçoise

If you are a traditionalist—especially if you are a French traditionalist—you probably want to just cruise by this recipe. It breaks some rules of the classic niçoise, like using salmon instead of tuna or anchovies, using normal green beans instead of fava beans, and adding some boiled new potatoes. I don't care so much about tradition in this case. The salad works, and the ingredients are all easy to find and easy to prepare.

Servings: 2 large salads | Prep Time: 20 minutes | Total Time: 40 minutes

Quick Herb Vinaigrette

1 teaspoon minced fresh thyme

1 tablespoon minced fresh basil

2 tablespoons minced shallot

¼ cup fresh lemon juice

⅓ cup olive oil

1 teaspoon Dijon mustard

Salt and pepper

2 large eggs

1 pound new potatoes

1 cup green beans, ends removed

½ head green lettuce

6–8 ounces (1 heaping cup) flaked cooked salmon

1 medium ripe tomato, cut into wedges

⅓ cup chopped kalamata olives

1 tablespoon capers

¼ cup sliced red onion

1. **For herb vinaigrette:** Make sure to mince fresh herbs very finely. If you are using dry basil and thyme, reduce thyme to ½ teaspoon and basil to 1 teaspoon. Whisk together herbs, shallot, and lemon juice. Drizzle in olive oil and whisk furiously to combine ingredients. Season with mustard, salt, and pepper. Alternatively, you can add the ingredients to a jar with a lid and shake it like crazy to mix together the dressing. Extra dressing will keep in the fridge for 2 weeks.

2. **For the salad:** First, hard boil the eggs. Add eggs to a medium pot and cover with cold water. The water should be at least 3 to 4 inches above the eggs. Set over high heat, cover, and bring to a boil. Once the water is boiling, turn off the heat, keep covered, and let eggs cook for 14 minutes.

3. You can use the same water to cook the beans and potatoes. Remove eggs, rinse in cold water, and set aside. Return the pot to high heat, season water with a big pinch of kosher salt, and return to a simmer.

4. When water is simmering, add potatoes and simmer until cooked through, about 10 minutes. Remove potatoes and add green beans. Blanch green beans until they are bright green and still slightly crispy, about a minute. Remove green beans and rinse with cold water to stop the cooking.

5. Peel hard-boiled eggs and cut the eggs into quarters. Roughly chop potatoes and cut green beans into 2-inch pieces.

6. Rinse and dry the lettuce, and chop it into bite-size pieces.

7. Split ingredients evenly on two plates, starting with lettuce and adding the cooked eggs, potatoes, and green beans, then the salmon, tomatoes, olives, capers, and red onion.

8. Drizzle dressing over salads. Start with just a tablespoon or two of dressing and then let people add extra dressing to their salads if desired.

Cucumber Sandwiches

This might go down as the fastest recipe in this entire book. But that doesn't mean that it isn't really tasty. Whatever you do, don't forget the mint. It totally makes the sandwich. Traditionally these sandwiches have the crusts cut off, but that's obviously not necessary. It just looks cleaner.

In my opinion, these little sandwiches work best as an appetizer or served with afternoon tea if that's your thing.

Servings: 4 as an appetizer | Prep Time: 15 minutes | Total Time: 15 minutes

1 large cucumber

8 ounces cream cheese

1 tablespoon minced fresh mint

½ teaspoon garlic powder

½ teaspoon granulated onion

8 slices white bread

4–6 ounces (1 scant cup) flaked cooked salmon

Kosher salt

Smoked paprika, for sprinkling

1. Run your vegetable peeler down the sides of the cucumber, leaving streaks of peeled cucumber alternating with streaks of non-peeled cucumber. Slice cucumber into thin rounds.

2. Mash together cream cheese, fresh mint, garlic powder, and granulated onion.

3. Cut crusts off bread and smear four slices with the cream cheese spread. Top with flaked salmon and then a layer of sliced cucumbers. Sprinkle cucumbers with kosher salt.

4. Top each sandwich with another piece of bread and slice sandwiches into quarters. Sprinkle sandwiches with smoked paprika and serve immediately.

Mint and White Bean Salad

If there's one tip I could give to people trying to use leftover fish effectively, it's to use fresh herbs and don't skimp on them. Big herbs like mint and dill work really well with seafood and can round out the fishy flavors nicely. There's a lot of mint in this quick bean salad. It's not a typo.

Personally, I think this salad is best with dried beans, but they do take some extra time to cook, so feel free to substitute with canned if you need to save some time.

Servings: 4–6 | Prep Time: 15 minutes | Total Time: 20 minutes

4 cups cooked cannellini beans or 2 (15-ounce) cans

½ cup slivered red onion

⅓ cup minced fresh mint

1 tablespoon olive oil

1 tablespoon fresh lemon juice

6 ounces (1 cup) flaked cooked salmon

Dash of hot sauce

Salt and pepper

1. If you're using dried beans, soak them overnight and then cook according to package instructions. Once they are cooked, drain them and measure out 4 cups of beans for the recipe. Two cups of dried beans should give you enough cooked beans for this recipe, but I always make a larger batch. You can also use two 15-ounce cans of white beans. If you use canned beans, drain and rinse the beans well with cold water.

2. Stir together red onions and mint with the beans. Add in olive oil and lemon juice. Fold in flaked salmon. Try to keep it in nice-size chunks.

3. Season salad with a dash of hot sauce, salt, and pepper.

4. Serve salad at room temperature, or chill and serve cold. The salad loses its fresh flavors after about 2 days in the fridge.

Salmon Croquettes

This is probably the most elegant way to present what is essentially a stuffed tater tot. If you serve these, people will be wowed. Anything fried is probably going to be good, but these are *really* good. Ideally, if you pair these with some leftover mashed potatoes, you can skip making the potatoes just for this dish.

Servings: About 20 croquettes | Prep Time: 20 minutes | Total Time: 1 hour

1 cup mashed potatoes, cooled

6 ounces (1 cup) flaked cooked salmon

½ cup sweet peas

2 scallions, minced

2 tablespoons minced fresh parsley

2 tablespoons lemon juice

Dash of hot sauce

Salt and pepper

2 large eggs, beaten

2 cups bread crumbs

2 quarts vegetable oil, for frying

1. Ideally, you would have some leftover mashed potatoes for this recipe, but if not, peel and cube a large russet potato and then boil it in lightly salted water until it's tender, about 10 minutes. Drain the potato and mash it with a few tablespoons of milk until it's nice and smooth. Season with a pinch of salt and pepper and let it cool.

2. Gently fold mashed potatoes together with flaked salmon, sweet peas, scallions, parsley, and lemon juice. Season mixture with a dash of hot sauce and a pinch of salt and pepper.

3. Beat eggs in a medium bowl. Pour bread crumbs into a second bowl. Use plain bread crumbs or the Japanese-style panko variety.

4. Working with the potato mixture, form heaping-tablespoon portions into fat cylinders (think tater tots). Once each croquette is formed, transfer it to the egg mixture to wet the exterior, then transfer straight to the bread crumbs and coat each croquette completely. Transfer finished croquettes to a baking sheet.

5. Heat two quarts of oil in a large pot until it reaches 350°F. When oil is hot, fry croquettes in batches until they are golden brown, about 6 minutes per batch.

6. When croquettes come out of the fryer, let cool for a few minutes on a plate lined with paper towels.

7. Serve croquettes while still warm. If you aren't going to serve immediately, you can keep cooked croquettes warm in a 200°F oven for 20 minutes or so.

S.O.S. (Salmon on a Shingle)

I spent about a year making breakfasts at a local homeless shelter once a week. I would wake up around 4:00 a.m. and cook for anywhere from fifty to one hundred people. I had a few popular dishes that people seemed to like, but one that always received good reviews was some version of S.O.S. (slop—or a different four-letter word—on a shingle), which is some sort of gravy on toast. It's filling and cheap to make. You can use almost any leftover meat in the cream sauce, but salmon is a particularly nice treat. This is comfort food at its best.

Servings: 2 | Prep Time: 10 minutes | Total Time: 15 minutes

2 tablespoons unsalted butter

2 tablespoons minced shallot

Kosher salt and pepper

2 tablespoons all-purpose flour

¾ cup warm milk

6 ounces (1 cup) flaked cooked salmon

4 pieces thick toast

Fresh parsley, garnish

Hot sauce, garnish

1. Add butter to a medium pot over medium heat. Once melted, add shallot and a pinch of kosher salt. Cook until shallot softens, about 2 minutes.

2. Whisk flour into butter mixture to form a roux. Cook for a minute until roux turns a light tan color.

3. Slowly whisk in milk. Turn heat down to low and cook until the mixture thickens, about a minute or two.

4. Stir in flaked salmon and season with salt and pepper.

5. Serve creamed salmon over thick toast and garnish with fresh parsley and hot sauce.

Pink and Green Penne

When I first met my wife, Betsy, it became pretty apparent that I would be the cook in the relationship. But she had a few meals that she would cycle through in any given week, and one of her favorites was a simple pasta salad with canned tuna, Granny Smith apples, and slivered almonds. It's actually delicious even if it sounds a bit strange. I adapted it for salmon and subbed pistachios for the almonds.

Servings: 4–6 | Prep Time: 20 minutes | Total Time: 30 minutes

1. Cook penne in nicely salted water (1 tablespoon kosher salt per gallon of water) according to package. Be careful to not overcook it.

2. Drain pasta and toss with olive oil, apples, and chopped pistachios.

3. Gently fold flaked salmon into the pasta while it's still warm. Season with salt, red pepper flakes, and ground black pepper.

4. Garnish with slivered fresh basil and serve immediately!

1 pound penne pasta

2 tablespoons good-quality extra-virgin olive oil

2 Granny Smith apples, cored and sliced thin

¾ cup chopped shelled, roasted, and salted pistachios

10–12 ounces (1½–2 cups) flaked cooked salmon

Kosher salt

½ teaspoon red pepper flakes

½ teaspoon ground black pepper

¼ cup slivered fresh basil

Chipotle Salmon Tacos

Reheating seafood is tricky business. It can dry out very quickly if you don't keep an eye on it. For this recipe, try to reheat the salmon in large pieces instead of flaked like many of the other recipes. Also, wrapping the salmon in foil and rubbing it with some oil keeps the moisture locked in.

These tacos just simply don't taste like leftovers. They are delicious, and you'd be crazy not to try them if you have some leftover fish.

Servings: 8 tacos | Prep Time: 20 minutes | Total Time: 30 minutes

1. Preheat oven to 350°F.

2. Rub salmon fillet with a drizzle of neutral oil and sprinkle with chipotle chile pepper and a pinch of kosher or sea salt. Wrap salmon loosely in foil and place on a baking sheet.

3. When oven is hot, bake salmon for 5 minutes, just to heat it through and infuse the chipotle flavor.

4. While salmon bakes, stir together sour cream, dill seeds, lime juice, and a pinch of salt for the sauce.

5. To heat the tortillas, add them to a dry skillet over medium-high heat for about 15 seconds on each side, just to warm them. Alternatively, if you have a gas stove, you can crank the burners on high and use tongs to lightly toast the tortillas for a few seconds on each side. Be careful if you use the open flame method, and make sure your stove is clean!

6. Add chopped spinach and flaked chipotle salmon to each tortilla. You should use a little over an ounce of salmon per taco. Top salmon with a drizzle of the lime dill sauce, red onions, Cotija cheese, and fresh cilantro. Serve immediately!

8–10 ounces (1½ cups) cooked salmon, whole fillet if possible

1 teaspoon neutral oil (canola or vegetable)

1 teaspoon dried chipotle chile pepper

Kosher or sea salt

Lime Dill Sauce

½ cup sour cream

½ teaspoon dill seeds

½ lime, juice only

Pinch of salt

8 fajita-size (6-inch) flour tortillas

1 cup chopped spinach

½ cup sliced red onion

4 ounces (about 1 cup) Cotija cheese, crumbled

¼ cup fresh cilantro, loosely packed

CHAPTER 14

BEEF STOCK

If you were to take a look inside my fridge at any given time, there's a very strong chance that you would see various containers of stocks: chicken, beef, and vegetable. For some reason it's the one thing that I can never remember if I have or not while shopping. So I inevitably buy more and then have two or three containers of stock in my fridge. I doubt I'm alone in this.

So this chapter is a collection of some of my favorite recipes that use varying amounts of stock. While I wrote it for beef stock—and I think the recipes work best with beef stock—any leftover stock from vegetable to chicken could be used for most of them, except for maybe the Bloody Mary and the Pho recipe. Those really do need beef stock specifically.

The next thing I'll say about this chapter is that it's undoubtedly better in the winter. Most of the dishes are hearty soups and stews that are just perfect on a cold winter night. It's not that you can't use the recipes in this chapter in summer, but I just prefer them during the colder months.

Also, the base recipe for this chapter, Roasted Beef Stock, is one of the few recipes in this book that I would categorize as advanced. It's not that any individual step is difficult, but it takes about two days and requires some ingredients (like beef bones) that you might not be used to buying. To make it right, it also requires some serious equipment like a large roasting pan and a large stockpot.

So it's important to remember that you don't need to make the recipes with homemade stock, although they all benefit from homemade stock. The recipe that I would argue benefits the most from homemade stock is the Forty Minute Pho recipe. Because it's mostly a broth, having a really good broth is pretty important.

I tried to give a variety of recipes in this chapter that use different amounts of stock. So if you have a lot, you can turn to the soup recipes, as they use at least a quart of stock. But then things like the Bulgogi Rice Bowl or Bangers and Mash use much less stock, so you can use up the end of a container.

This is one chapter where I really encourage substitutions. Feel free to experiment substituting different stocks that you have on hand. And if you have a free weekend and are feeling ambitious, give the Roasted Beef Stock a shot. It's pretty amazing.

Roasted Beef Stock

When you have a really good soup at a restaurant, chances are that it has a stock base very similar to this. It's a completely different product than what you find in stores. The final product has a deep, rich color and flavor. It's just impossible to replicate unless you take the time.

This is obviously not a spur of the moment-type recipe. You don't just throw this together in an afternoon. It takes some planning and two full days to do it right, but the final product will rock your socks. Also, this recipe isn't necessarily cheap. To make good stock requires a lot of beef bones, which aren't as cheap as you might think. It's worth it though, if you have the time.

Servings: Makes 8–10 cups of stock | Prep Time: 20 minutes | Total Time: 2 days (5 hours roasting, 3 hours simmering, 1 hour the following day)

6 pounds beef bones (marrow bones, shanks with bones, or oxtail)

1 pound beef stew meat

¼ cup olive oil

2 teaspoons kosher salt

1 teaspoon coarsely ground black pepper

5 large carrots, chopped into thirds

5 stalks celery, chopped into thirds

1 large white onion, quartered

4 cloves garlic, crushed

14–16 cups water

3 egg whites plus shells, for clarifying

1. Preheat oven to 350°F.

2. Toss bones and stew meat with olive oil and season well with salt and pepper. Put bones and meat in a large roasting pan with high walls, as there will be a lot of fat that melts off. A normal baking sheet will not work.

3. Roast the bones for 3 hours, stirring them once halfway through.

4. Add carrots, celery, onions, and garlic to the roasting pan. Return pan to oven and roast for another 2 hours.

5. Add contents of roasting pan to a large stockpot (I use a 12-quart pot). You could use two smaller pots, but really one large pot is ideal.

6. Add 1 cup water to the roasting pan and use the liquid to scrape up any bits stuck to the pan. Add that to the stockpot also.

7. Fill the stockpot with water until it covers the bones by about an inch. Make sure to use at least 14 to 16 cups of water; you might need more depending on your pot.

8. Bring the stock to a simmer over high heat. Reduce heat to medium and let the stock simmer for 3 hours, partially covered. During this simmer time, check on the stock occasionally to make sure it's simmering and not boiling over. Also, if a lot of foam accumulates on top of the stock, skim it off.

9. Once stock has simmered for 3 hours, remove from heat and let cool for an hour or so until stock is warm, but not boiling hot.

10. Pour stock through a wire mesh strainer into a large bowl. Try to filter out as many of the solids as possible.

11. Store stock in the fridge overnight.

12. The next day, use a large spoon to carefully scoop congealed fat off the top of the stock.

13. Once most of the fat is skimmed off, add stock back to a large pot (now you can use a normal 4-quart pot). Heat stock until it is almost simmering.

14. In a bowl, whisk together egg whites until they start to form peaks. Then crunch eggshells into bits and whisk them into the whites.

15. Add eggs to the stock mixture and stir vigorously to distribute eggs in the stock. Allow to simmer slowly for 15 minutes. It shouldn't be at a rapid boil, but the water should be circulating. The purpose of this step is to clarify the stock and remove a lot of

Note: When you pour off the liquid, don't throw away the bones without first picking the meat off. It's very good in quesadillas, tacos, or added to many of the recipes in this chapter. Save and shred the stew meat as well.

the bits in it. If you boil the stock vigorously during this step, it won't work. Just keep it at a slight simmer.

16. After 15 minutes, the eggs and shells will have latched on to the debris in the stock and formed a sort of raft on the top of the stock. Pour the stock through a strainer lined with cheesecloth. That should filter out much of the debris in the stock and leave you with a fairly clear stock. It's okay if it's not perfect.

17. Store the stock in the fridge for up to 10 days or freeze for up to 6 months.

Note on collagen: Because this stock is made with lots of bones, it will have a fair amount of natural collagen in it. As the stock cools, it might thicken slightly even after you skim off the fat. Don't worry about it! As soon as you reheat it, it will liquefy again and be as good as new. If it is very thick, you can add some water to thin it out, but don't add too much as it will also dilute the flavor.

Beefy Bloody Mary

This is a fun little recipe I first made on a whim one morning when I was in the mood for a brunch cocktail and had some leftover beef stock in my fridge. The stock really ups the savory flavors in the drink. Because of this, you can leave out the Worcestershire sauce that normally goes in Bloody Mary mixes.

Servings: Makes about 56 ounces of mix, enough for 8 drinks | Prep Time: 10 minutes | Total Time: 10 minutes

1. **For the mix:** Whisk together tomato juice and beef stock, then whisk in lemon, horseradish, hot sauce, pepper, celery salt, and kosher salt. Feel free to taste and adjust to your liking. I like mine on the spicy side and typically add an extra tablespoon of hot sauce.

2. You can pour the mix back into the tomato juice bottle for storage, but it won't all fit, so you'll have to make a drink right away. Too bad.

3. **To make a Bloody Mary:** Fill a large glass with ice. Add Bloody Mary mix and vodka and stir well. Garnish with celery, olives, or a pickle slice.

4. Store the mix for up to 7 days in the fridge or freeze it for later. If you freeze it, make sure the container isn't filled completely or it might explode.

Bloody Mary Mix

46 ounces tomato juice (from concentrate is fine)

1 cup beef stock (homemade is best)

1 large lemon, juice only

2 tablespoons grated horseradish

1 tablespoon hot sauce, or to taste

1 tablespoon freshly ground black pepper

2 teaspoons celery salt

1 teaspoon kosher salt

One Bloody Mary

6–8 ounces mix

2–3 ounces vodka

Celery

Olives

Pickle

Forty Minute Pho

Extremely good pho takes a lifetime to get right, which is why many good pho shops serve almost nothing else. I'm not pretending that this will be the best pho in the world, but think of it as Pho 101—an introduction.

If there's any recipe in this chapter that I encourage you to use homemade stock for, it's this one. If you use store-bought stock, let it simmer for a bit longer with the aromatics to get some extra flavors going. Once you have the stock done, this recipe only has a few pieces. To be honest, forty minutes is an overestimate of the amount of time it should take to throw it together.

Servings: 4 | Prep Time: 15 minutes | Total Time: 40 minutes

Broth

4 cups beef stock

2 cups water

4 inches fresh ginger, sliced

4 whole cloves

1 cinnamon stick

2 tablespoons fish sauce

1 tablespoon sugar

Add-ins

12–16 ounces sirloin steak, slightly frozen

4 scallions, chopped

1 red chile, sliced thin

Fresh cilantro

Fresh mint

12 ounces rice noodles

½ cup bean sprouts

Sriracha chili sauce

Lime wedges, garnish

1. Add all the ingredients for the broth to a medium pot and bring to a simmer. Cover and simmer for 10 minutes. The longer you simmer this, the more flavor will be infused. If you're using store-bought stock, feel free to add more flavors to this simmer, such as some onion, carrot, celery, and garlic.

2. Slice your steak into very thin slices. This is easier if you put the steak in the freezer for 30 minutes. Chop the scallions, red chile, cilantro, and mint.

3. Cook noodles according to package in a separate pot. Don't cook them in the broth, as it will make the broth too thick.

4. While the broth is still simmering, add the bean sprouts to the broth for just 5 seconds so they heat up and blanch slightly. Remove them.

5. Right before serving, blanch the steak slices in the simmering broth. I dunk my steak slices in the very hot broth for just 10 seconds, which should be enough time to start to cook the very thin slices. They will continue to cook as they sit in the bowl—and you don't want to overcook them.

6. Distribute hot, cooked noodles between bowls. Top noodles with slightly cooked steak slices. Ladle hot broth over the steak and noodles.

7. Top pho with vegetables and herbs. Garnish with chili sauce and lime wedges. Serve immediately!

Poblano Chile Soup

You would think this soup has tons of ingredients in it, but it gets most of its flavor from roasted poblano peppers. As they roast, their flavor becomes really intense. You could leave this soup chunky, but I like to blend it so it has a smoother consistency.

Whatever you do, don't forget the tortilla strips. They completely make the dish. In a pinch you could just toss some tortilla chips on top.

Servings: 4–6 | Prep Time: 20 minutes | Total Time: 1 hour

4 large poblano peppers

2 tablespoons olive oil

1 cup chopped white onion (about 1 medium onion)

2 cloves garlic, minced

2 tablespoons chili powder

1 tablespoon ground cumin

½ teaspoon dried oregano

Salt and pepper

4 cups beef stock

2 cups water

1 (14-ounce) can diced tomatoes

1 tablespoon fresh lime juice

12 ounces frozen sweet corn

Cilantro, garnish

Lime wedges, garnish

Corn strips, garnish

1. Preheat oven to 450°F.

2. Roast poblano peppers, turning once, until they are nicely blistered all over, 20 to 25 minutes. Remove peppers from oven and place in a bowl. Cover with plastic wrap and allow to steam for 10 minutes.

3. Meanwhile, add olive oil to a large pot over medium heat. Add onions and garlic and cook until veggies start to soften, about 5 minutes.

4. Add chili powder, cumin, oregano, and a pinch of salt and pepper and cook until the spices are very fragrant, about 30 seconds.

5. Add stock, water, and tomatoes to the pot and bring to a simmer.

6. Once peppers have steamed, try to remove the skin from the peppers. Most of it should easily rub off, but don't worry about the peppers being perfectly clean. Cut off stems and remove seeds from peppers, then roughly dice.

7. Add three-quarters of the diced peppers to soup and continue to simmer for 10 minutes. Reserve the rest for topping the soup later.

8. Use an immersion blender to blend the soup until smooth. If you don't have an immersion blender, you can use a normal blender, but allow the soup to cool for a few minutes, and don't fill the blender completely full (blend in batches) or it might overflow!

9. Once soup is mostly smooth, return to medium heat and continue to simmer. Season with lime juice and salt and pepper. Finally, add frozen corn and cook until corn is hot, about 2 minutes.

10. Serve soup garnished with reserved roasted poblano peppers, cilantro, lime wedges, and corn strips.

11. **For corn strips:** Slice six to eight corn tortillas into ½-inch strips. Bake the strips until they are very crispy and slightly browned, 8 to 10 minutes.

Beef Barley Stew

If there's another meal out there that I would rather have on a cold night, it doesn't come to mind. This stew is thick and wholesome and will leave you feeling warmed and cozy. It's peasant food at its base with potatoes, turnips, and carrots, but I would happily serve this to the POTUS if he happened to be at my table in January.

When serving, don't skimp on the Greek yogurt and parsley. They make the flavors really come alive.

Servings: 6 | Prep Time: 20 minutes | Total Time: 1 hour 20 minutes

1. Cube beef into ½-inch pieces. Season beef cubes with a pinch of salt and pepper. Add 3 tablespoons oil to a large, heavy pot (at least 5 quarts—a large dutch oven works well) over medium-high heat. Add half of the beef and brown for 8 minutes, stirring once halfway through. Brown the beef in two batches so as not to crowd the pan.

2. Remove beef from pan and add chopped leeks and carrots. Cook until leeks are softened, about 4 minutes. Use a heavy spoon to scrap up any bits as the leeks cook. Turn the heat down to medium if the leeks start to burn.

3. Add the potatoes, turnips, bay leaves, red pepper flakes, and a big pinch of black pepper to the pot. Finally, add beef back in. Stir well to combine and then add beef stock and water. Bring to a simmer.

4. Once simmering, add barley and turn heat down to medium low. Simmer, partially covered, until barley is cooked and soft, about 40 minutes. Stir every 10 minutes or so to avoid burning anything on the bottom of the pan. If ever the stew looks dry, feel free to add more liquid, but the 8 cups of total liquid should be enough.

5. Before serving, remove bay leaves and taste the stew for salt and pepper. It will probably need at least a pinch of salt.

6. Serve the stew garnished with a dollop of Greek yogurt (or sour cream) and freshly chopped parsley.

2 pounds beef chuck roast

Kosher salt and pepper

3 tablespoons olive oil

2 cups chopped leeks (about 2 medium leeks)

1 cup chopped carrots

2 medium red potatoes, ½-inch cubes

2 cups chopped turnips (1 large turnip)

2 bay leaves

½ teaspoon red pepper flakes

1 quart beef stock

1 quart water

1 cup pearl barley

Greek yogurt or sour cream, garnish

Fresh parsley, garnish

Bulgogi Rice Bowl

This is a good shared recipe with the Rice chapter. If you have some stock and cooked rice, this dish can be made with very little effort.

Be sure to follow the instructions carefully about removing any liquid that accumulates as you cook the beef and then adding it back at the end mixed with the other sauce ingredients. Also, the longer you can let the beef marinate the better, but I've had good flavor even with just thirty minutes.

Servings: 4 | Prep Time: 15 minutes plus marinade time | Total Time: 45 minutes plus marinade time

1½ pounds sirloin steak

Bulgogi Sauce
½ cup beef stock
¼ cup soy sauce
2 tablespoons toasted sesame oil
1 tablespoon brown sugar
¼ cup peeled and minced fresh ginger (about a 3-inch piece)
1 tablespoon Sriracha chili sauce
2 teaspoons cornstarch

1 tablespoon vegetable oil
1 cup shredded carrots
½ cup thinly sliced red onion
4 ounces (about 3 loosely packed cups) fresh spinach
Cooked rice for serving
¼ cup sesame seeds (I like a mix of black and white), garnish
Kimchi, garnish (optional)

1. Stick steak in the freezer for 30 minutes, then slice very thinly across the grain of the meat.

2. In a medium bowl, whisk together the ingredients for the Bulgogi sauce that will be used as a marinade: stock, soy sauce, sesame oil, brown sugar, ginger, and chili sauce.

3. Add sliced steak to sauce to marinade. Let sit for at least 30 minutes, but overnight would be best.

4. When ready to cook, remove beef from marinade, keeping as much of the marinade as possible in the bowl (you'll use it later). Pat beef pieces dry with a few paper towels.

5. Put a large wok or skillet over high heat. Once hot, add vegetable oil. When oil is shimmering, add beef and fry quickly for about 3 minutes per side. The pieces should be so thin that they cook very quickly.

6. When beef is cooked (maybe 5 or 6 minutes), pour off any liquid that has accumulated in the pan so the pan is mostly dry. In a small bowl, add your leftover marinade sauce from earlier and enough of the cooked beef drippings to equal 1 cup. Whisk cornstarch into the sauce/drippings bowl.

7. Add shredded carrots and onions to the wok and stir to combine. Cook with beef for about a minute.

8. Add the sauce with cornstarch mixture to the wok. Let simmer until sauce begins to thicken, about 30 seconds.

9. Stir in the spinach, which should wilt almost immediately.

10. Serve beef and veggies over rice in large bowls. Garnish with sesame seeds and kimchi.

Three Mushroom Risotto

If you read my website often, you'll know that I have a serious bone to pick with restaurants that overcharge for risotto. It's rice! People think it's some exotic dish that's impossible to prepare, when the reality is that it's very achievable for most home cooks, even on weeknights. Master homemade risotto and then save your bucks for other things when you go out to eat.

If you can't find the exact mushrooms I used in my version, feel free to experiment with other mushroom varieties.

Servings: 4–6 | Prep Time: 30 minutes (mostly inactive) | Total Time: 1 hour 15 minutes

¾ ounce dried shiitake mushrooms

¾ ounce dried porcini mushrooms

4 cups boiling water

4 cups beef stock

3 tablespoons olive oil, divided

1 pound (about 5 cups) fresh cremini mushrooms, sliced thin

Salt and pepper

1 cup diced white onion (about 1 medium onion)

1½ cups Arborio rice

½ cup white wine or lager beer

½ cup shredded Parmesan cheese

2 tablespoons minced fresh basil

1. Add boiling water to dried mushrooms in a medium bowl and let sit for 30 minutes to reconstitute. Remove mushrooms and wring them out to press out as much liquid as possible. Then roughly chop mushrooms and reserve for later.

2. Add the liquid from the mushrooms to a large pot along with beef stock and bring to a low simmer.

3. In a large skillet over medium heat, add 2 tablespoons olive oil. Once hot, add sliced cremini mushrooms and a pinch of salt. Cook until mushrooms lose their moisture and are slightly browned, about 8 minutes. Remove mushrooms and combine with reconstituted mushrooms.

4. Add onions to the pan along with another tablespoon of oil if the pan is dry. Cook until onions start to soften, 3 to 4 minutes.

5. Add rice to the pan and cook for 2 minutes, stirring constantly.

6. Add wine or beer to the pan and use the liquid to scrape up any bits that are stuck to the pan.

7. Once wine or beer has evaporated, start ladling in hot stock in ¾-cup increments. As you add the stock, slowly stir the risotto so the liquid is evenly distributed. You don't need to constantly stir risotto, as is often said, but you do need to keep an eye on it and stir it regularly.

8. When the pan is dry, add more hot stock and continue to stir until the rice grains are cooked through but still have a slight bite to them. Depending on your pan, your heat, and a few other factors, this will most likely take 6 to 8 cups of stock and probably around 30 to 40 minutes. Taste the risotto as it cooks to test for doneness.

9. When the rice is soft but still has a tiny bite to it (not mushy), stir in all the cooked mushrooms. Cook for another few minutes to combine flavors, then season the risotto with salt and pepper.

10. Top risotto with shredded Parmesan cheese and freshly chopped basil and serve immediately!

Bangers and Mash

The first time I had this dish was at a small hole-in-the-wall in Brighton, England. It can often be a bit on the dreary side there, and when we visited it was a chilly night. This was the perfect meal to warm me up.

You might think that the key to this dish is the sausage selection, but I would beg to differ. I think the real key is the gravy. I've made this dish over the last few years with a few different kinds of sausage, and it's always great as long as the gravy is good.

Servings: 4 | Prep Time: 20 minutes | Total Time: 45 minutes

2 pounds red potatoes

4 tablespoons unsalted butter

⅔ cup milk

2 cloves garlic, minced

Salt and pepper

5 ounces raw baby spinach

1 tablespoon olive oil

8 medium sausage links

Onion Gravy

1 sweet yellow onion, sliced thin

2 tablespoons unsalted butter

2 tablespoons all-purpose flour

2 cups beef stock

1 teaspoon sugar

1 teaspoon balsamic vinegar

Pinch of salt and pepper

1. **For the mash:** Cube red potatoes into 1-inch cubes. Leave the skin on.

2. Simmer in boiling water until potatoes are very soft, about 15 minutes.

3. Drain potatoes, then add them back to the hot pot with butter, milk, and garlic. Mash until smooth and season with salt and pepper. Cover and keep warm until needed.

4. **For the spinach:** Add rinsed and dried spinach to a large skillet over medium heat and drizzle with oil. Cook for a minute or two until spinach starts to wilt. Remove from heat and set aside until needed. You don't need to keep it warm.

5. **For the bangers and gravy:** Preheat oven to 250°F.

6. Add sausages to a medium pot over medium-low heat with a small drizzle of oil. Cook slowly until the sausages are browned on all sizes. If you cook them too fast, they might burn on the outside but still be raw in the center. So take your time and cook them on slightly lower heat.

7. After 20 minutes or so, the sausages should be cooked. Remove from pot and keep them warm in the oven until ready to serve.

8. Add sliced onions to the pot that you cooked the sausage in. Add butter and turn up heat to medium. Use juices from onions to scrape up any sausage bits stuck to pan. Cook until onions are soft, 5 to 6 minutes.

9. Add flour to pan, stir, and cook for about a minute to cook out flour taste.

10. Whisk in beef stock and bring to a simmer. It should thicken slightly and become a light gravy.

11. Stir in sugar and vinegar and continue to simmer until gravy is the right consistency. It should thicken slightly, but still be a bit thinner than a traditional gravy. Season gravy with salt and pepper.

12. **To serve:** Add a big scoop of mashed potatoes to the plates. Top with sautéed spinach and add a big ladle of onion gravy. Top each plate with two sausages and a bit more gravy. Serve immediately!

Beef Stroganoff

My generation was the beef stroganoff generation. I had it often as a kid, and it involved cans of soup. That's all I can honestly remember about it. This version is kind of a different beast. The thing that confuses me about the soup version is that it doesn't really save you that much time and pretty much makes the dish a gloopy mess. In this version, the flavors are clean, if that makes sense. Serve it over buttered egg noodles always and forever.

Servings: 4 | Prep Time: 20 minutes | Total Time: 40 minutes

4 tablespoons unsalted butter, divided

1 pound sirloin steak, sliced into thin pieces

1 medium white onion, minced

8 ounces (about 3 loosely packed cups) cremini mushrooms, sliced thin

Salt and pepper

½ cup drained diced tomatoes

1 cup beef stock

1 tablespoon Dijon mustard (optional)

12–16 ounces egg noodles

⅔ cup sour cream

Freshly chopped parsley, garnish (optional)

1. Put a large pot of water on to boil to cook egg noodles in later.

2. Melt 1 tablespoon butter in a large skillet over medium-high heat. Once melted, add sliced beef and let it brown well on all sides. This should take 2 to 3 minutes per side. Remove beef from pan.

3. After beef is browned, add onions and mushrooms to skillet with 2 more tablespoons butter and cook for a few minutes until veggies are tender and mushrooms have lost their liquid. Season with a pinch of salt and pepper.

4. Add diced tomatoes, stock, and optional mustard, and use liquid to scrape up any bits that might be stuck to the pan. Turn down heat to low and simmer for a few minutes.

5. Cook egg noodles according to package. Drain them, return them to the hot pot (but turn off the heat), and stir in a tablespoon of butter to coat the noodles.

6. Add beef back to pan with sauce and stir in sour cream. Simmer for another minute or two.

7. Serve stroganoff over noodles and garnish with fresh parsley.

CHAPTER 15

ICE CREAM

When I started planning this book, I really wanted to include a dessert chapter, but I was having a hard time thinking of something that was easily adaptable for multiple desserts. The answer was right under my nose. Or, I guess, right in my freezer.

You see, I have a mild ice cream problem. It's one of my "unlimited foods," meaning I can eat an almost unlimited amount of it. I have absolutely no problem killing a quart of ice cream in a day or two. I have to pace myself when it comes to the frozen stuff.

While there are plenty of decent store-bought ice creams on the market, and all of those can be used for the supporting recipes in this chapter, there's something wonderful about a creamy homemade vanilla ice cream.

Most ice cream manufacturers actually churn a lot of air into their ice cream, which makes it light and fluffy. That can be good sometimes, but homemade ice cream is thick, rich, and decadent. It's something that I make for special occasions because if I made it regularly, I would likely weigh a quarter ton.

When it comes to actually eating ice cream, I'm normally a purist. I like vanilla. And I like a lot of it. Nothing fancy. But change is always good, and all of the supporting recipes in this chapter are excellent ways to change up dessert. They are also a smart way to stretch a small amount of ice cream a long way.

So bust out the ice cream maker, go buy some bulk vanilla beans, and get churning!

Vanilla Bean Ice Cream

Homemade ice cream gets a bad rap for being (A) difficult and (B) expensive.

The truth is, making ice cream at home isn't that hard once you have a few key pieces of equipment. Obviously you'll need an ice cream maker of some sort. There are a bunch of different makes and models, and they all essentially do the same thing. Look for one with positive reviews on Amazon and make sure it holds at least a quart of ice cream.

Besides the ice cream maker itself, I also think it's helpful to have a nice mesh strainer, which will help to strain out the custard for the ice cream. This will make for a much smoother finished product.

The first time you try to make homemade ice cream, you might think that it's a huge process. I promise that if you do it a few times, it will become really easy for you. These days I can rock out a batch of homemade vanilla ice cream with just a few minutes of work.

As far as expense, it's true that homemade ice cream can be more expensive, but it all depends on quality of ingredients. Remember that cheap brands of ice cream are cheap because they use cheap ingredients (high fructose corn syrup, artificial flavors, and so on). You probably won't be able to beat these brands on cost. But you can easily beat them on flavor. Quality brands of ice cream can easily cost $6 to $8 per quart, which we can match or beat at home.

Servings: Makes about 1 quart | Prep Time: 20 minutes plus steeping time | Total Time: 45 minutes plus chilling time

1 vanilla bean

2 cups whole or 2% milk

¾ cup sugar

Pinch of salt

6 large egg yolks

2 cups heavy cream

1 teaspoon vanilla extract

1. Slice vanilla bean in half lengthwise and scrape out seeds with a knife. Add seeds and bean to a medium saucepan with milk, sugar, and a pinch of salt. Bring to a light simmer over medium-low heat. Be careful not to scald milk.

2. Remove milk mixture from heat and let sit for 1 hour to steep. This isn't a completely necessary step if you're in a hurry, but it will result in better flavor.

3. Whisk together yolks in a separate bowl. Remove vanilla beans from steeped milk and bring milk mixture back to almost a simmer over medium heat.

4. Once hot, slowly whisk about 1 cup of the milk mixture into the yolks to raise their temperature. Then whisk all the hot yolks back into the saucepan.

5. Cook the custard mixture on low heat, scraping and stirring regularly with a heat-resistant spatula. Cook until the custard thickens and coats the back of a spoon, about 8 to 10 minutes. The custard should register about 170°F.

6. In a separate bowl, add cream and vanilla extract. Use a metal mesh strainer to strain warm custard into the cream mixture. This will remove any accidentally cooked egg.

7. Stir well to combine and chill mixture. You can either set it in your fridge for a few hours or set the bowl in an ice bath and stir for 8 to 10 minutes.

8. Once custard is cold, add to your ice cream machine and churn according to the instructions that came with your machine.

9. Once ice cream is a soft serve consistency, freeze until solid. I like to stir my ice cream once or twice as it freezes to break up ice crystals and make the finished texture very smooth.

Buttermilk Ice Cream

This is one of my favorite variations on a traditional ice cream and actually results in a lighter consistency that might be closer to a sherbet. The method is basically the same as the vanilla ice cream, but the buttermilk gives the final product a really nice, tangy flavor.

While I've provided the basic recipe below, I highly recommend trying this ice cream with any kind of stone fruit (peaches are my favorite). Just add about a cup of finely chopped fruit near the end of the churning process. The sweetness from the fruit is perfect with the tangy buttermilk.

This is definitely ice cream that you can't find in the store!

Servings: Makes about 1 quart | Prep Time: 20 minutes | Total Time: 1 hour plus chilling time

2 cups milk (whole is best)

1¼ cups sugar

8 large egg yolks

2 cups buttermilk

Pinch of salt

1 tablespoon vanilla extract

1. Add milk and sugar to a medium saucepan and bring to a light simmer.

2. Whisk yolks in a separate bowl.

3. Slowly whisk about 1 cup of the hot milk mixture into the yolks to temper them. Then whisk all the yolks back into the hot milk mixture.

4. Cook the custard mixture on low heat, scraping and stirring regularly with a heat-resistant spatula. Cook until the custard thickens and coats the back of a spoon, about 8 to 10 minutes. The custard should register about 170°F.

5. In a separate bowl, add buttermilk, salt, and vanilla extract. Use a metal mesh strainer to strain warm custard into the buttermilk mixture.

6. Stir the mixture until combined and chill. You can either set it in your fridge for a few hours or set the bowl in an ice bath and stir. That will cool it down very quickly.

7. Once custard is cold, add to your ice cream machine and churn according to the instructions that came with your machine.

8. Once ice cream is a soft serve consistency, freeze until solid. As mentioned, you can add any fruit you like just before freezing. I like to stir my ice cream once or twice as it freezes to break up ice crystals and make the finished texture very smooth.

Four Ice Cream Variations

These variations all begin with the basic vanilla ice cream recipe, but they are a bit more exotic. Use the ingredients listed instead of the original recipe ingredients. Any preparation changes are noted. You definitely can't find these in the store. The one exception is pistachio. While you can find pistachio in the store, the homemade version is much more flavorful.

VARIATION	INGREDIENTS	PREPARATION
Chocolate Chili Ice Cream	2 cups milk ¾ cup sugar Pinch of salt ¼ cup cocoa powder 2 teaspoons chili powder 6 large egg yolks 1 teaspoon vanilla extract 2 cups heavy cream	Add cocoa powder and chili powder to milk mixture and whisk well. Bring to a simmer. No need to steep mixture before whisking with egg yolks. Important to strain this custard before chilling and churning it.
Pistachio Ice Cream	1 cup pistachios ¾ cup sugar 2 cups whole milk Pinch of salt ½ teaspoon almond extract 6 large egg yolks 1 cup heavy cream ¾ cup pistachios, roasted and chopped	Grind 1 cup pistachios with sugar in a food processor. Add to milk, salt, and extract in a saucepan. Bring to a simmer. No need to steep the mixture before combining with the egg yolks. Strain the custard into the heavy cream and chill well before churning. Add final ¾ cup chopped pistachios near the end of the churning process.
Orange Ginger Ice Cream	2 cups milk ¾ cup sugar Pinch of salt 1 tablespoon minced crystallized ginger 6 large egg yolks 1 teaspoon vanilla extract 1 teaspoon orange extract 2 cups heavy cream ½ cup orange juice	Make custard mixture as you would with the standard recipe. Add ginger to the milk at the beginning of the recipe so it dissolves as the milk heats. Steep and stir the milk until most of the ginger dissolves. Reheat custard mixture if it has cooled, then strain custard mixture into cream. Add extracts and chill. Add orange juice before churning. **Note:** It's very important to add the OJ last or the acid could curdle the dairy.
Coconut Honey Ice Cream	2 cups milk ½ cup honey ¼ cup sugar Pinch of salt 6 large egg yolks 1 (13.5-ounce) can coconut milk 1 teaspoon vanilla extract	Make custard as normal, adding honey to the hot milk mixture with a pinch of salt. Once custard is thick, strain into coconut milk and add extract. Chill and churn!

Four Quick Ice Cream Sauces

The really nice thing about all of these sauces is that they take just minutes to prepare. You can make them on a whim, assuming you have the ingredients handy.

I love all of these over plain vanilla ice cream, but obviously you can create some fun combinations. Try the fresh strawberry sauce with the orange ginger ice cream, for example.

Making a simple, warm, homemade ice cream sauce makes ice cream a special occasion and a real treat. These sauces also happen to keep pretty well, for at least a week or two in the fridge. To reheat, just stir in a few tablespoons of water or milk and warm them up again on the stove over low heat.

VARIATION	INGREDIENTS	PREPARATION
Fresh Strawberry	2 cups fresh strawberries, halved ⅓ cup sugar 2 tablespoons water 1 teaspoon vanilla extract ½ lemon, juice only	Combine ingredients in a small saucepan over medium heat. Bring to a simmer and mash strawberries. Let simmer for 10 minutes until it thickens, stirring frequently. Serve warm or cold.
Peanut Butter	½ cup creamy peanut butter ½ cup milk 2 tablespoons cream 2 tablespoons sugar ½ teaspoon vanilla extract	Combine ingredients in a small saucepan over low heat. Stir until combined and smooth. Do not simmer or the sauce will break. When the sauce is warm and a single, slightly thick consistency, it's done. Serve warm. If your sauce does break and turn grainy, you can usually fix it by stirring in a few tablespoons of milk.
Dark Chocolate	1 cup heavy cream 1 cup dark chocolate chips ¼ teaspoon vanilla extract	Combine ingredients in a small saucepan over low heat until chips are melted. Sauce should be very thick, perfect for ice cream. Serve warm.
Marshmallow	⅓ cup milk or cream 1 cup marshmallows, about 8 large 1 teaspoon vanilla extract 1 tablespoon sugar	Combine ingredients in a small saucepan and heat over medium-low heat, stirring frequently. As marshmallows melt, they will start to foam. Watch it closely at this point, and once the marshmallows are completely melted, kill the heat. The sauce will thicken as it cools. Let cool a minute before using, but serve warm.

Ice Cream Sandwiches

One of my favorite ways to extend ice cream is to smash some of it between a few baked cookies. Personally, I like to use really good chocolate chip cookies, but almost any cookie will do the trick.

Regardless of what cookie recipe you use, I recommend making your cookies slightly smaller than you might normally make them, since there will be two of them and a few tablespoons of ice cream per sandwich. The other trick to these is to make sure you actually cool and freeze the cookies separately before making the sandwiches!

Servings: 12 sandwiches | Prep Time: 20 minutes | Total Time: 1 hour plus freezing time

1. Mix together dry ingredients (flours, salt, baking powder, baking soda). Set aside.

2. Cream together butter and sugars in a mixing bowl. If you are using a stand mixer, use the paddle attachment, or use a hand mixer. Mix in the egg and stir in vanilla extract.

3. Slowly add in dry ingredients. Once dry ingredients are mixed in, add chocolate chips and stir just until they are evenly distributed. Try not to overmix.

4. At this point you can chill the dough for up to 2 days. Or you can make the cookies immediately. If you want to make them now, preheat oven to 350°F.

5. To bake, scoop heaping tablespoon-sized balls onto baking sheets lined with parchment paper. You should get about 24 cookies out of the batch. Bake the cookies until they are lightly browned, but still somewhat soft, about 10 to 12 minutes.

6. Let cookies cool completely (preferably on a wire rack).

7. Once your cookies are cooled, transfer them to a large container and freeze for about an hour.

8. Sandwich a few tablespoons of ice cream between two cookies. Eat immediately or wrap sandwiches individually in plastic wrap, transfer to a freezer-safe dish, and freeze for up to 2 months.

4¼ ounces cake flour (1 cup minus 1 tablespoon)

4¼ ounces bread flour (1 cup minus 2 tablespoons)

¾ teaspoon table salt

¾ teaspoon baking powder

⅔ teaspoon baking soda

⅔ cup unsalted butter

½ cup brown sugar

¾ cup sugar

1 large egg

1 teaspoon vanilla extract

6 ounces chocolate chips

2–3 cups ice cream, for filling

The Banana Split

This is a classic, and it's definitely worth mentioning. Of course, the fun part with banana splits is the toppings! You can go crazy adding the toppings. The good news is that if you make them at home, you don't get charged by the topping.

Servings: 2, or 1 banana split | Prep Time: 5 minutes | Total Time: 5 minutes

1 large banana

3 scoops ice cream

1 or 2 homemade ice cream sauces (see page 250)

Whipped cream

Nuts or other toppings

1. Slice banana in half down the middle and place each half on the side of a large bowl, facing one another. Right in the middle, add a few scoops of ice cream.

2. Top ice cream with one or two homemade sauces. I particularly like strawberry and chocolate. Top with lots of whipped cream, nuts, and any other toppings you can imagine!

Twenty Delicious Toppings

Almonds

Andes mints

Berries (any kind)

Butterscotch

Candy sprinkles

Caramel sauce

Chocolate chips

Cinnamon Toast Crunch cereal

Coconut shavings

Granola

Lemon zest

Mango, fresh

Mint leaves

Maraschino cherries

Oreo cookies

Peaches, fresh

Peanuts

Pineapple, crushed

Vanilla wafers

Walnut

Dessert Parfait

I think this dessert gets the "most bang for your buck" award. It's a beautiful presentation and absolutely delicious, but it takes literally just a few minutes to make. I recommend taking the time to make a small batch of homemade whipped cream for these guys, but it's by no means necessary. Feel free to use a premade version.

Servings: 2 | Prep Time: 5 minutes | Total Time: 10 minutes

1 tablespoon sugar

1 cup heavy whipping cream

1 teaspoon vanilla extract

½ cup graham crackers

1½ cups ice cream

1 cup various berries (I like raspberries and blueberries)

1. In a cold metal mixing bowl, combine sugar, cream, and vanilla and whisk until cream forms stiff peaks. You can also use a mixer to beat the cream until it's whipped. (You could use any number of store-bought whipped creams, but I'm a big fan of homemade.)

2. Crush graham crackers with your hands.

3. In each of two tall glasses, add a small scoop of ice cream, about ¼ cup. Cover the ice cream with a dollop of whipped cream, a spoonful of crushed graham crackers, and a few berries.

4. For the second layer, add another small scoop of ice cream, more whipped cream, more graham crackers, and more berries.

5. For the top layer, add a final small scoop of ice cream. Top the parfait with whipped cream, more graham crackers, and a few berries.

6. Serve immediately!

Individual Ice Cream Cakes

These are incredibly fun and easy to make. You can make them with absolutely any ice cream flavor you might imagine. Once you make a tray or two of them, you'll have cute little individual desserts already portioned out and ready to serve.

Servings: 6 cakes | Prep Time: 10 minutes | Total Time: 15 minutes plus freezing time

1. For graham cracker crumbs, you can either pulse them in a food processor until they are ground or put them in a bag and mash them with a rolling pin (or something else heavy). You can also buy just the crumbs, although they are a bit more expensive.

2. Mix together graham cracker crumbs, butter, and a pinch of salt in a small bowl. Set aside for later.

3. Line a muffin tin with plastic wrap. Be sure to work the plastic wrap into each individual tin as well as you can.

4. Scoop in about ⅓ cup ice cream into each muffin tin. It helps if your ice cream is softened a bit so it flows easily into the cracks.

¾ cups graham cracker crumbs

2 tablespoons unsalted butter, melted

Pinch of salt

2 cups ice cream, any variety

1 cup heavy whipping cream

2 teaspoons sugar

1 teaspoon vanilla extract

Sprinkles

5. Freeze the muffin tin for at least 30 minutes.

6. Remove the muffin tin and pack on about 2 tablespoons graham cracker mixture onto each ice cream cake. Pack it down densely.

7. Freeze again for at least 30 minutes. If you plan to freeze for longer, cover with another layer of plastic wrap.

8. When you are ready to serve, whip together heavy cream, sugar, and vanilla extract in a cold metal bowl until it forms stiff peaks (you can also use a store-bought version).

9. Carefully peel out one of the ice cream cakes and invert it on a plate. Completely cover cake with a layer of whipped cream.

Hint: If you add a dollop of whipped cream under the cake, it won't slide around while you frost it.

10. Cover with sprinkles and serve immediately!

Choco-Peanut Shakes

A rich and thick milkshake is one of my absolute favorite desserts. Actually, sometimes I like to go crazy and have one with a burger, but that's neither here nor there. The point is this: When you have a quart of nice homemade ice cream in your freezer, you can really take your milkshakes to the next level. Below are the proportions for one of my personal favorite shakes, but also try any toppings from the Banana Split (see page 254). Go crazy!

Servings: 2 milkshakes | Prep Time: 5 minutes | Total Time: 5 minutes

1. Add ice cream to a blender. Scoop in peanut butter. Pour in milk, vanilla extract, and cocoa powder.

2. Blend until smooth. Add more milk if the shake is really thick or you just want it thinner.

3. Pour into two tall glasses and top with whipped cream and any of the optional toppings.

2 cups ice cream (vanilla works best)

⅔ cup peanut butter

1 cup milk

1 teaspoon vanilla extract

¼ cup cocoa powder

Whipped cream

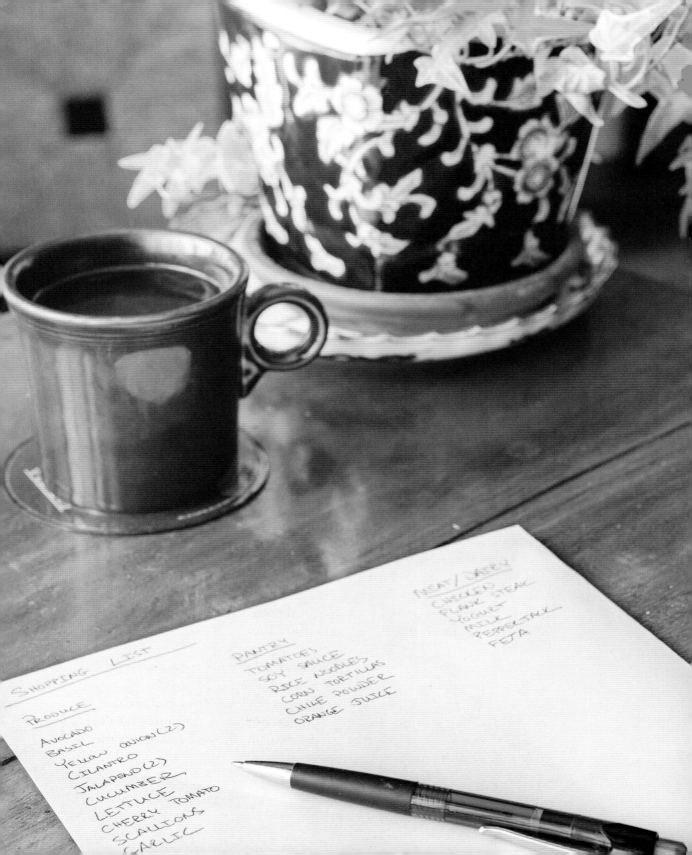

SHOPPING LIST

PRODUCE
Avocado
Basil
Yellow Onion (2)
Cilantro
Jalapeno (2)
Cucumber
Lettuce
Cherry Tomato
Scallions
Garlic

PANTRY
Tomatoes
Soy Sauce
Rice Noodles
Corn Tortillas
Chile Powder
Orange Juice

MEAT/DAIRY
Chicken
Flank Steak
Yogurt
Milk
Pepperjack
Feta

CHAPTER 16

MEAL PLANNING 101

Part of the reason I'm excited about this book is because I've heard from so many people over the years who are decent, or even exceptional, cooks, but who struggle with meal planning. The two skills absolutely do not come naturally together. You have to practice cooking to become better at it, and you have to practice planning to become better at it. While my goal with this book is to give you some great recipes to structure your meal plans around, I thought it would be helpful to give some very specific strategies that I use and also provide a few sample meal plans to get you started!

Ten Meal Planning Tips I Use

1. **Take Five.** Literally. I like to take five minutes before I even jot down a recipe or list just to think about the upcoming week. This might sound silly, but I find that it helps to make it an actual pointed activity. I think about what days might be busier and therefore I'll have less time to cook. Are there any social activities where I'll be eating dinner? Is it anybody's birthday (do I need to make a cake)? It does no good to create a fantastic meal plan for the week only to remember on Wednesday that you have to go out for a work-related dinner.

2. **Same time. Same place.** For me, it's Sunday morning with a second cup of coffee. I always block off twenty to thirty minutes a week to plan what my cooking schedule will be for the upcoming week. I can almost promise you that my cooking schedule is more intense than yours needs to be, so you might be able to get away with less time. It doesn't matter when or where, but try to find a time of the week that works well for you and plan your meals during that time every week.

3. **Monday through Sunday.** I recommend actually using the calendar week to plan your meals. Personally, I use an electronic calendar for this, but a paper calendar might work better for you. You can share the calendar with your family so they can get excited about upcoming meals! Whatever you use, actually write out the days for the week and what you plan to have each day.

4. Recipe source. I wish I could tell you how many times I've looked at my meal plan and saw something like "veggie lasagna" on the dinner schedule for the night. The only problem is that I know approximately one hundred different veggie lasagna recipes. Which one was I thinking of five days ago when I made this meal plan? Nobody knows! The point is that if you're using specific recipes, write the source (and page number if it's a cookbook) next to the recipe so you can find it easily later.

5. Note the season. It's very trendy to say that you are eating seasonal produce, but the truth is that it can save you money and make your meal planning easier. For example, if it's February and I'm making a marinara sauce, I'm not even going to check the produce section for tomatoes. I know they won't be good enough for a sauce base. I'll just add a few cans of tomatoes to my list. On the other hand, if it's August, I'll do the opposite and probably be able to find wonderful tomatoes for cheap.

6. Check before you check out. Before you head out for the store, spend a minute to run through your list and cross-check it with what's in your fridge and pantry. You will almost certainly find a few things already on hand that you didn't know about. I'm chronically bad at this step. Betsy once presented me with four different containers of couscous. I'm working on it!

7. List by store. If you do all your shopping at one grocery store, then this won't be an issue. For me, I sometimes go to three or four different stores in a week. If I just made one master list, I would forget what I was supposed to pick up at each place. To solve the problem, I make one big list but sort it by store.

8. List by category. I've seen some people get as crazy as making their shopping lists by store aisle. That's a bit much for me, but I do like to categorize my lists by basic areas. I'll make a list for produce, meat, dairy, pantry, and everything else. When I say pantry, I mean stuff like flour, canned goods, and spices.

9. Have a backup plan. I can pretty much guarantee that at least once a month (if you're very good) something will go wrong with your meal plan. Try to have a backup plan in place that isn't fast food. For us it's frozen burritos. We make them in bulk using leftovers like chicken or turkey, freeze them, and then reheat them if we are in a dinner bind.

10. **Relax!** Cooking should be fun, and while meal planning isn't always the most fun part of the week, there's no need to stress about it. You're working to make good meals for you and your family, and you should feel good about it.

The Art of the Side Salad

When it comes to making new meals out of leftovers, I often use a side salad to fill the gaps on the plate. It doesn't need to include everything in the produce section, but it shouldn't be the exact same thing every day or your eaters will get bored. Below is the formula I use to make a huge range of delicious side salads.

A Green Base

Not all salads have a lettuce component, but I find that for quick dinner side salads it's easiest to start with a nice bed of some sort of green. You can buy pre-mixed and pre-washed greens these days, which makes this step incredibly easy, but if you are looking to save some money, buy the greens in bulk. Personally, I rotate between spinach, green leaf lettuce, red leaf lettuce, and kale (diced very finely). If I'm buying something like beets, I'll wash the green tops of the beets well and use them for greens in salads. I stay away from iceberg lettuce because I think it tastes kind of bland without a lot of other toppings and dressings.

Rotating Vegetable Base

This is one thing I don't write on my shopping list, but when I'm out and about I keep my eyes open for three or four good crunchy, non-starchy vegetables that I can easily stack onto my lettuce base. Some of my favorites include celery, carrots, ripe tomatoes, green or red peppers, radishes, raw beets (peeled and diced small), red onions, scallions, broccoli florets, red cabbage (shredded), snap peas, fresh corn, zucchini, and squash.

Fun Toppings

Besides the base, I try to add one or two fun toppings to the salad to make it interesting. This is where you can really go crazy. Cheese is an easy out here, but I try to avoid it, especially if other parts of the dinner involve cheese. Some of my favorite toppings include avocado, slivered almonds, sprouts, apples, cashews, currants, granola, olives, pears, pomegranate seeds, pistachios, and watercress.

The House Dressing

I haven't bought salad dressing in probably five years. It's so easy to make at home, and it's a great way to save some money. Also, most store-bought dressings use fairly cheap ingredients. There are a few dressing recipes scattered throughout this book (see the Steakhouse Salad on page 47 and the Sesame Salad on page 162), but below is my standard dressing recipe that I almost always have at the ready in our house. There is no chopping or anything complicated involved in this dressing recipe. You can mix up a batch in under a minute. If you don't have a salad dressing jar, you can use an old mustard jar. Just shake all the ingredients together really well.

½ **cup neutral oil (Something like sunflower, safflower, or even canola. Olive oil has too strong a flavor.)**

¼ **cup tarragon vinegar (No substitutions! It's in your vinegar section. Find it. Okay? But apple cider vinegar is pretty good too.)**

¼ **cup sugar or honey**

1 **teaspoon kosher salt or ½ teaspoon table salt**

1 **teaspoon ground pepper**

½ **teaspoon hot sauce (I like Cholula, but any hot sauce will work.)**

Four Sample Meal Plans

In general these meal plans should feed four people for dinner five days of the week. This leaves plenty of room for schedule adjustments. They are intended as a starting point and to give you some ideas for how you can use the recipes in this book to flesh out a weekly meal plan.

MEAL PLAN ONE: STEAK AND POTATOES

Day One: Grilled Flank Steak (see page 42) and Basic Baked Potatoes (see page 60) with side salad.
   Plan Ahead: Grill an extra flank steak and bake five pounds of potatoes. That will most likely leave you with two to three pounds of flank steak and eight to ten potatoes left over.
   Meal Time: 1 hour 15 minutes

Day Two: Steakhouse Salad (see page 47). This is a really hearty salad, and I think it works great as a meal.
   Meal Time: 15 minutes

Day Three: Weeknight Gnocchi (see page 72). Serve with a salad or garlic bread.
   Plan Ahead: Make a double batch of the Basic Red Sauce; use half to accompany the gnocchi and the other half for a pizza sauce later in the week.
   Meal Time: 45 minutes

Day Four: Vietnamese Noodle Salad (see page 54). It's okay if you don't have quite enough steak to make a full batch of this. It's plenty filling with even half the steak in the recipe. You'll probably have leftovers of this also, which are great the next day for lunch.
   Meal Time: 30 minutes

Day Five: Potato Pizza (see page 76). Use homemade or store-bought crust. Use leftover marinara sauce thinned with a bit of water and blended as a quick pizza sauce.
   Meal Time: 30 minutes plus homemade crust prep if you go that route.

MEAL PLAN TWO: LENTILS AND BREAD

Day One: Green or red lentils (see Basic Lentils, page 100) with Roasted Garlic Bread (see Four No-Knead Bread Variations, page 118). Try adding some of the fun add-ins to the lentils you plan to eat that night.

Plan Ahead: Make two pounds of lentils so you have plenty for other recipes.

Meal Time: 1 hour 30 minutes plus overnight rise for bread

Day Two: Ten-Minute Lentil Wraps (see page 103).

Meal Time: 10 minutes, no joke

Day Three: Grilled or roasted chicken and Sun-Dried Tomato Panzanella Salad (see page 121).

Any grilled chicken recipe goes very well with this salad.

Meal Time: 45 minutes

Day Four: Chorizo Bread Soup (see page 128).

Meal Time: 45 minutes

Day Five: Seared Salmon with Caper Lentils (see page 108) with side salad.

Meal Time: 30 minutes

Note: If you still have leftover lentils, try out the Lentil Cookies (see page 113) for an interesting dessert!

MEAL PLAN THREE: SALMON AND RICE

Day One: Herb-Roasted Salmon (see page 208) and rice (see page 186) with side salad.

Plan Ahead: Bake an extra side of salmon (about two pounds) and cook at least a pound of rice so you have plenty left over.

Meal Time: 35 minutes

Day Two: Pink and Green Penne (see page 221) with a side salad.

Meal Time: 30 minutes

Day Three: Chipotle Salmon Tacos (see page 223) with chips and salsa.

Meal Time: 30 minutes

Day Four: Arroz Mixto (see page 201, double recipe for four) is one of my favorite midweek fast dinners.

Meal Time: 20 minutes

Day Five: Chicken and Rice Soup (see page 197) with garlic bread or just crackers and/or a side salad.

Meal Time: 45 minutes

Note: If you have any rice at all left from this week, please make the Coconut Rice Pudding (see page 204) for a dessert treat. I think it's my favorite recipe in that chapter.

MEAL PLAN FOUR: PULLED PORK EXTRAVAGANZA

This four-day meal plan will work best if you plan non-pork meals in between a few of the days. Otherwise you can get a bit sick of pulled pork, even though it is delicious and each dish is unique.

Day One: Grilled (or Roasted) Pork Butt (see page 134) sandwiches with Sriracha Slaw (see page 139)

Plan Ahead: Just follow the recipe! Seven to eight pounds of delicious pulled pork will give you more leftovers than you know what to do with.

Meal Time: 10 hours. It is what it is.

Day Two: Snap Pea and Pork Stir-Fry (see page 153).

Meal Time: 40 minutes

Day Three: Banh Mi (see page 145, doubled for four). A different take on pork sandwiches that will taste very different from the day-one sandwiches.

Meal Time: 20 minutes

Day Four: Pulled Pork BBQ Pizza (see page 142) with a side salad.

Meal Time: 30 minutes plus homemade dough prep if you decide to try that.

Note: Even with these four days of meals, you might still have pulled pork left over. You can seal it tightly and freeze it for later.

ACKNOWLEDGMENTS

This book is by far the most substantial single project I've ever taken on in my life. There's no way I could've finished it without a lot of help.

First, a big shout-out to my wife, Betsy. She's always my biggest supporter and harshest critic. Both roles are very important when you're trying to write a book. She also tries almost everything I cook, which is not always an easy job! Thanks also to my animals, Porter the Wonderdoodle and Tipsy the Cat, for sitting by me while I wrote and cooked. Thanks for never running away during the cursing.

Thanks to my longtime friend and first-round editor, Liz Kinsley, who allowed me to contract out her very expensive English education for practically nothing. Thanks to Jeff Warner for helping me with some of the headshot photos and accepting only beer as payment. Also, a huge thanks to my agent David Dunton and to my editors Lara Asher and Julie Marsh, plus all the other Globe Pequot staff, for helping me bring this project to life.

Thanks to my parents, who are very supportive even though I'm not entirely sure they understand what a "blog" is.

Thanks to the following lovely people who spent their time and money helping me test the recipes in this book. Almost every recipe in this book was somehow improved by their comments. In no particular order: Paul K., Heather L., Lisa H., Adrienne B., Jessica H., Stacie C., Dianna G., Kathleen O., Mandy L., Jean G., Kenneth M., Kiyomi B., Allison M., Claire and Ben E., Amy S., Steve J., Doug C., Matthew K., Julie and Matt K., Barb G., Peggy G., Niki C., Melissa R., David S., Katie G., Alyson M., Kelley R., and Mary A.

And finally, thanks to you for spending your hard-earned money on what I hope becomes a very weathered and dog-eared cookbook on your shelf.

INDEX

RECIPE KEY:

Q—Quick. Under 30 minutes

V—Vegetarian

B—Betsy's Favorite—Betsy is my official taste-tester. With very few exceptions, she tries everything I cook. She also has exceptional taste evidenced by the fact that she married me.

ABOUT THE AUTHOR

NICK EVANS has been writing about cooking for the last five years on his cooking blog, Macheesmo.com. He is a featured writer for tablespoon.com and does recipe development for food companies like Muir Glen and Cascadian Farms. His Macheesmo recipes have been featured on a variety of sites, including *Serious Eats, The Huffington Post,* and *America's Test Kitchen.* Nick graduated from Yale University with a degree in philosophy and lives in Denver, Colorado, with his wife and official taste-tester, Betsy, their dog, Porter, and their cat, Tipsy.